PROJECTION
STENCILING

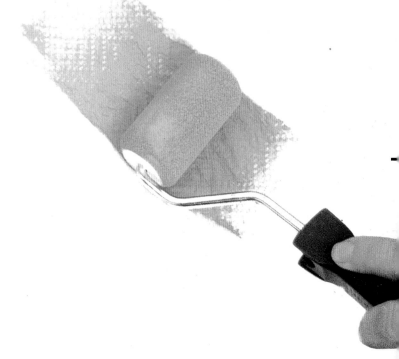

PROJECTION
STENCILING

LINDA BUCKINGHAM ✦ LESLIE BIRD

Hartley & Marks
PUBLISHERS

Published by
HARTLEY & MARKS PUBLISHERS INC.
P. O. Box 147   3661 West Broadway
Point Roberts, WA   Vancouver, BC
98281   V6R 2B8

ISBN 0-88179-180-6

Book design by Supriti Bharma.
Composition by John McKercher of The Typeworks
Photographs by Ken Mayer, KM Studios; Lionell Trudell;
Ingeborg Suzanne Hardman, Oceanview Photography

Set in ITC STONE, POETICA, and COCHIN

Printed in Hong Kong

NOTE TO THE READER

As with any endeavor, when you embark on a painting or stenciling project, take the proper health
precautions. To protect yourself from chemicals, including paints, wear a mask and safety goggles.
This is especially important when using sprays. Be particularly careful when cutting with an X-acto or
utility knife. Make sure your fingers stay well clear of the cutting path. Use gloves when handling
chemicals and paints. Neither the authors nor the publisher can take legal or medical responsibility for
persons using this book.

This book is dedicated, with love,
to my little brother and our friend,
Bill Buckingham, whose contribution to
our book, in both spirit and
man hours, was enormous.

Contents

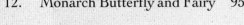
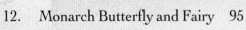
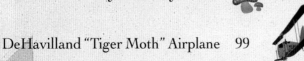

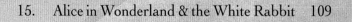

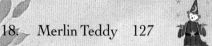

Acknowledgments

The putting together of this book has been a long process—but the journey along the way has been made lighter by many people. We are indebted to Vic Marks, our publisher, and Susan Juby, our editor, for their belief in our concept. Susan was patient, ever-smiling, and extremely helpful in keeping us on track. We would like to give a special thanks to all the friendly staff at Hartley & Marks Publishers. Our hats are off to John McKercher, our tireless typesetter, for his enthusiasm and patience, and Rocky Ingram, production manager, for all his help. We would also like to thank Supriti Bharma for combining the words and photographs to create a beautiful completed work. Thanks to Edward Turner for his sketches and illustrations, Marian Robinson, a wonderful artist and friend, for many of the illustrations in this book, and Sue Emerick for her artistic advice.

Thanks to Sandra Buckingham for the generous sharing of her ideas and thoughts and for proofreading the initial text. Thanks to Georgina King, friend and decorative painter who has embraced the projection technique, helped us with many seminars, and contributed her cave art work for our book. Thanks to the helpful staff at The Bay, Vancouver Downtown, and the staff at Country Furniture. Thanks to my daughter, Dana Savage, for doing preparatory work and pitching in whenever I needed a hand.

Thanks to David Haynes, Pat and George Shore, and Susan and Michael Ritzker for the generous use of their homes for photo shoots and to Georgene McKenzie, owner of Delicado's. Thanks to David Haynes, Toni Vance, Ford White, Helen Maclachlan, Ingo and Madeline Neil St. Claire, and Barb's Country for the use of furnishings and props for the photographs and to David Haynes and Helen Maclachlan for assistance in setting up for the photo shoots. And of course, thanks to Frank, our dog model, and to Dolcé, the fearless feline stealing his dinner.

Thanks to the photographers—Ken Mayer, Lionel Trudell, and Ingeborg Suzanne Hardman—who managed to fit into tiny spaces and make Christmas in July believable.

Thanks to my brother, Bill Buckingham, for his countless hours of computer graphics work, even through the discomfort of three broken ribs. His unfaltering belief in the projection process from its inception inspired our self-confidence and creativity.

Linday thanks her husband, Greg Deacon, for his unconditional support and belief in her endeavors. Leslie thanks David Haynes, her partner, for pitching in wholeheartedly whenever she needed help and for uplifting her spirits.

And finally, thanks to our parents, Pat and George Shore, and Audrey Bird, for their support and love.

10 ▶

Introduction

*A*s decorative painters, my friend and business partner, Leslie, and I see the world differently than most people. For us, potential stencils lurk everywhere. Such was the case with the photo of a wrought iron headboard I found in a magazine. The headboard's clean and simple lines begged to be stenciled. I had never undertaken such a large stenciling project before and, had I guessed at how mammoth a project it would become, I may never have begun. Leslie and I measured, marked, and taped the straight bars of the design. Once these were stenciled and shaded, we again measured, marked, and taped the shadows. The process was quickly becoming tedious, and we still had the most challenging part ahead of us — figuring out how to draw the design for the curved and rounded parts of the headboard. Seized with inspiration, I grabbed a garden hose, pie plate, and dinner plate and used them as templates to draw a design on freezer paper. Once I drafted the design it was only a simple matter of affixing it to the wall with a repositionable spray glue, cutting out the openings, and stenciling them in.

The result was sensational! Everyone who saw the headboard believed it was real and needed to touch it to convince themselves otherwise. My house at the time was filled with stenciling and faux finishing, but the thing that people exclaimed over more than anything else was the headboard. Leslie and I were onto something with this new kind of stencil, but didn't know how to simplify the technique. We estimated that it took over fourteen hours to complete the headboard, and we could see few people willing to invest that amount of time and effort in a stencil, no matter how spectacular the result.

We knew there had to be an easier way and, sure enough, there was. A few days

later, while wandering around our favorite art supply store, Leslie and I spotted an Artograph "Tracer." Intrigued, we took a closer look at the little projector powered by a hundred-watt light bulb. Immediately we thought, "That's it! There's the key to making large stencils!" And we split the cost of the Tracer and fought over who got custody. Our much-loved Tracer spent the next two years going back and forth between our two homes. I was granted sole custody when Leslie found the bargain of a lifetime at a secondhand store—a new Tracer for $3.99!

And that is how the idea for this book was born. We will show you how you can leave the dishes in the cupboard, the hose in the yard, forget about tedious full scale drawings, and still achieve great results. All it takes is a basic knowledge of stenciling and the willingness to embark on a creative adventure.

PART 1

Projection Stenciling

*P*rojection stenciling is a new method for
creating both large and small stencils. It can be
used to paint wall murals, produce faux "inlay,"
"etch" beautiful window designs, stencil floorcloths,
and in fact, stencil just about any surface. We use
the term "projection stenciling" rather loosely since
we have found our technique to work equally well
on smaller projects. The term now refers to a
method of transferring or projecting a design onto
stenciling paper using a light projector, grid system,
or photocopy, and cutting out the stencil directly on
the surface to be painted. Projection stencils look
hand painted. Our "inlaid" (stenciled) woodwork
fools seasoned workworkers and our "etched" glass
is a dead ringer for the real thing. In traditional
stenciling a stencil is put down, paint is applied, and
then the stencil is repositioned for the next repeat.
In this way a design is built around the room, one
repeat at a time. In projection stenciling there is no
repeating. A piece of paper is sprayed with repositionable spray adhesive and then placed on the wall
or object. The design is then traced onto the paper,
using one of the enlargement methods described in
Chapter 2. Each design element is color-coded, as in
paint-by-numbers, and all the pieces of one color

◄ 15

are cut out with an X-acto® knife or a sharp utility knife (with snap-off blades), leaving these areas exposed and ready for stenciling. Once one color is stenciled in, another color portion is cut out and stenciled. The pattern pieces for the first color may need to be replaced before the next color can be stenciled to avoid "bridges," gaps in a design that are a telltale sign of stenciling. Projection stencil designs are built one color at a time. It is as simple as that. If you can follow a color-coded illustration and are familiar with the basics of stenciling, you are ready to start projection stenciling.

STENCIL MADNESS:
THE WHERES & WHERENOTS OF STENCILING

There is a tendency for stenciling enthusiasts to overdo it. And while we don't suggest you get too carried away, it is true that just about any surface can be stenciled. My husband and I recently sold our family home which had stenciled walls, ceilings, floors, furniture, and closet doors. We now live on a boat and when I first moved aboard, I looked at the mahogany walls and thought, "Not much room for stenciling here." Now, several months later, our new home boasts stenciled curtains, "etched" windows, cabinet glass (see page 197), and mirrors, an "inlaid" wood coffee table (see page 186), and an inlaid wood panel on the refrigerator (seee page 184). I stenciled a floorcloth for the galley (see page 220), and my next project will be placemats for the dining table.

Opportunities for stenciling are everywhere and almost any surface can be stenciled, including drywall, wood, fabric, glass, tile, linoleum, and concrete. Projects can be as simple as a motif painted in the corner of a mirror, or as complex as a mural encompassing an entire room. Stenciling looks great in bedrooms, bathrooms, living rooms, kitchens, foyers, and laundry rooms. And stenciling need not be confined to the interiors of a home. It can be applied in a variety of settings, including restaurants, daycares, recreational facilities, nursing homes, retail outlets, hotels, and hospitals. Leslie has created stencils in some very unlikely places. On her hands and knees she transformed the concrete floor of a fish hatchery into river rocks. Balancing on a makeshift scaffolding she changed a curved staircase into a savannah setting for a herd of life-sized zebras. And standing on a twenty-foot ladder she stenciled a desert sunset scene on large display boards for a building supply store.

Of course, we are not advocating stenciling every surface in your house or your community. On the contrary, it's important to carefully select a project and place it so that it enhances and complements your environment rather than clutters or competes with it.

If you are a beginning stenciler interested in projection projects, you can practice stenciling with commercial stencils or those cut from freezer paper. Follow our step-by-step instructions and familiarize yourself with roller and brush stenciling. Start stenciling on paper and graduate to walls as your confidence grows. Some safe places to practice stenciling are inside closets, the laundry room, or inside the garage.

Once you have mastered basic stenciling, you are ready to begin your first projection project. Start small. Rather than trying to set the tone or the mood of the room with your project, use it to provide an accent or accessory to the general decor. By beginning with small projects, you will familiarize yourself with projection stenciling and gain the confidence to move on to more complex projects.

As you progress to larger, more challenging projects ensure that your artwork fits into its surroundings. For example, the carousel pony on page 80 might look a bit lost placed in isolation on a wall in a child's bedroom. But combining the pony with balloons and a canopy creates a whole ambience. The same is true with the zebras on page 46, where a field of dried ferns stenciled around the base of the room provide a sense of continuity.

Another way to ensure your stenciled project looks like it belongs in your room is to stencil it within the boundaries of an object or an architectural feature. Stencil a scene on the front of a dresser, on closet doors, or in a recessed part of a wall. It is far easier to incorporate a mural of limited scope into its surroundings than it is to use a whole wall. If you don't have suitable natural boundaries in your room, create the illusion of one by stenciling a window or a door. The cottage window on page 152, the cypress tree on page 148, and the Greek scene on page 158 show how effective it can be to create the illusion of an opening in a wall to frame a mural.

If you are renting or "not allowed" to paint on your walls, you have several options. You can move, change partners, restrict yourself to small projects, paint your murals on movable structures (large panels, folding screens, blinds, canvases), or you can do what I do. When my husband seems less than enthusiastic about a proposed project, I wait until he goes out of town and then proceed as planned. On his return, he is invariably pleased with the results. In fact, I have noticed that if he is particularly taken with a project, he begins to think it was his idea. Leslie overcomes the problem of stenciling resistance by being very selective about the men she dates. Experience has taught her that her prospects must not only appreciate her decorative painting, they must also be willing and able to apply a good base-coat.

CHAPTER 1

Stenciling Basics

efore you embark upon any of the projects in this book, you need to learn the basics of stenciling. A stencil is a thin template which can be made from a variety of substances such as mylar, cardboard, metal, or paper into which a design has been cut. Stenciling is the art of applying paint or stains through the openings in the stencil. There are two basic methods for applying paints or stains: roller stenciling and brush stenciling. Leslie and I are often asked to give stenciling demonstrations at retail and trade shows. Usually we begin these demonstrations by stenciling fern fronds on our easel. One of us takes the largest stenciling brush we have (one inch) and the other takes our stenciling roller. Then we race to see who can stencil the fastest. By the time the one with the brush has completed one print, the other has filled the easel with ten prints. Now we really have our audience's attention! Not only does the roller always triumph, but the prints it produces are easily as good, if not better, than the brush prints. This is because the roller method lends itself to even paint coverage and natural shading. We do use stencil brushes for small cutouts and for very

controlled shading, but the bulk of our stenciling is done with stenciling rollers.

ROLLER STENCILING
TOOLS AND MATERIALS

Paint

A variety of paints are suitable for roller stenciling, including household latex paint. Craft acrylic paints require an extender or retarder to be used effectively for roller stenciling. They come in an endless variety of colors, can be purchased in small quantities, and are widely available. An extender is a product that retards the drying time of paint, thus allowing it more "open time." We recommend adding about 20% extender to craft acrylic paint to make it suitable for roller stenciling. The paint we used throughout this book was mainly

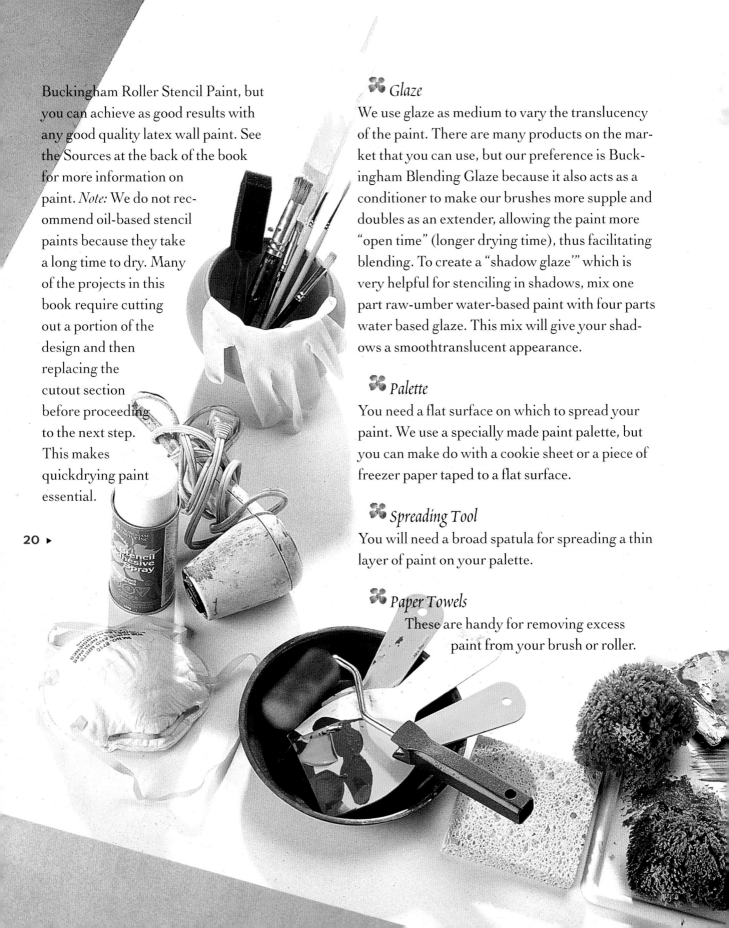

Buckingham Roller Stencil Paint, but you can achieve as good results with any good quality latex wall paint. See the Sources at the back of the book for more information on paint. *Note:* We do not recommend oil-based stencil paints because they take a long time to dry. Many of the projects in this book require cutting out a portion of the design and then replacing the cutout section before proceeding to the next step. This makes quickdrying paint essential.

❀ Glaze

We use glaze as medium to vary the translucency of the paint. There are many products on the market that you can use, but our preference is Buckingham Blending Glaze because it also acts as a conditioner to make our brushes more supple and doubles as an extender, allowing the paint more "open time" (longer drying time), thus facilitating blending. To create a "shadow glaze'" which is very helpful for stenciling in shadows, mix one part raw-umber water-based paint with four parts water based glaze. This mix will give your shadows a smoothtranslucent appearance.

❀ Palette

You need a flat surface on which to spread your paint. We use a specially made paint palette, but you can make do with a cookie sheet or a piece of freezer paper taped to a flat surface.

❀ Spreading Tool

You will need a broad spatula for spreading a thin layer of paint on your palette.

❀ Paper Towels

These are handy for removing excess paint from your brush or roller.

❧ Stencil Adhesive

This is a low-tack repositionable glue that you spray on the back of your freezer paper so that it lies securely against your surface to be stenciled. Make sure you have adequate ventilation when you use this product. *Note:* It is important to let the glue dry for a few minutes before placing the paper on the wall. If you find your wall is still a bit sticky after you remove your freezer paper, let the stencil dry for a few days, then moisten a clean rage with paint thinner (not alcohol) and very lightly rub the wall surface. This will remove any lingering tackiness fromthe spray adhesive, should there be any.

❧ Freezer Paper

Freezer paper, or butcher's paper as it is also known, is a brown or white paper coated on one side with a thin film of plastic. The untreated (or dull) side of the paper is sprayed with adhesive and the treated (or shiny) side is used for stenciling. Freezer paper is ideal for the projects in this book because it is easy to cut with an X-acto® knife or utility knife (with snap-off blades), comes in large rolls, and is readily available at almost any supermarket or butcher shop.

❧ Stenciling Rollers

You need a high density foam roller. Soft foam or nap rollers hold too much paint and won't allow you to get a clean print. We use Buckingham Stencil Paint rollers which are custom-made for stenciling. The handles are perfectly balanced for even paint distribution, and the foam heads have rounded ends to minimize paint lap lines.

ROLLER STENCILING TECHNIQUE

✿ Step 1

Squirt a dollop of paint onto one end of your palette.

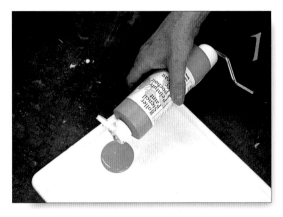

✿ Step 2

Use your spreading tool to draw out a long, thin film of paint.

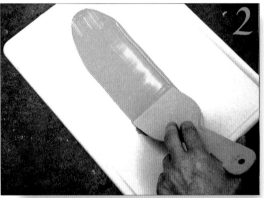

✿ Step 3

Start with a dry roller and roll it through the full length of your drawn-out paint. The whole roller should be lightly loaded. Now roll your roller back and forth vigorously several times (without picking up additional paint) to evenly distribute the paint.

✿ Step 4

This is the most important step, so be careful here. Roll your roller back and forth several times on a paper towel or old terry towel to remove excess paint. You will be surprised at how little paint you need. Stenciling, whether with a brush or a roller, is almost a "no paint" method. If you run your roller over your hand you will see very little paint.

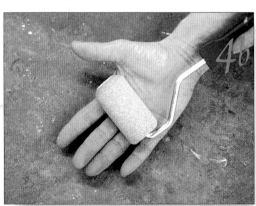

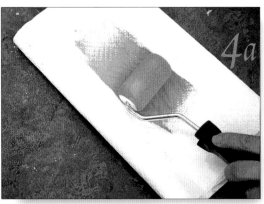

🍀 Step 5

Before stenciling your image, practice on a sheet of scrap paper. If you don't have a stencil to practice with, make one by cutting any simple shape out of the center of a piece of freezer paper. Spray the stencil lightly on the back (the matte side) with stencil adhesive, allow it to dry for a few minutes, then press the stencil onto paper. Run the roller back and forth across the whole stencil, pressing lightly at first. Build up the paint gradually for more depth of color.

Hint: You may find the paint on your roller is drying and starting to feel sticky. Roll it lightly back and forth over a damp kitchen sponge to "revive" the paint. Then work your roller back and forth on the palette without picking up more paint.

Hint: Prevent your roller from drying out when you take a break by putting it into a small Ziplock® bag.

BRUSH STENCILING

There are two ways to stencil using a brush: a swirling technique and a stippling technique. To use the swirling technique, rub your paint through the opening in the stencil using a circular motion. To use the stippling technique, apply the paint by "pouncing" or dabbing your brush up and down. We generally find the swirling technique faster and easier.

TOOLS AND MATERIALS

🍀 Stenciling Brushes

Choose good quality stencil brushes. Make sure the bristles are soft, supple, and densely packed. If they are too stiff you won't achieve the smooth, even buildup of color that is the hallmark of good stenciling. Stencil brushes usually range in size from ¼" to 1" in diameter. Use large brushes to stencil large openings, small brushes to stencil small openings, and a combination of brush sizes for shading.

Note: Generally when we stencil large openings we use the roller stenciling method described on page 22 and reserve brush stenciling for shading and highlighting our designs. For additional tools and materials, refer to Roller Stenciling Tools and Materials on pages 19–21.

BRUSH STENCILING TECHNIQUE

🌸 Step 1

Pour a small amount of glaze onto your paint palette (Figure 1a). Pick up a small amount of glaze on your brush and work it in well to condition the brush (Figure 1b.) Wipe off the excess on a paper towel.

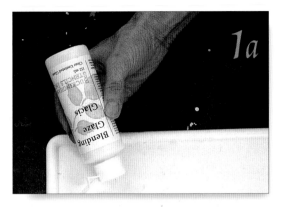

🌸 Step 2

Pour a dollop of paint onto your palette. If you want the paint to appear opaque, dip your brush directly into the paint. If you wish your paint to appear more translucent, add additional glaze to your brush before you dip it in your paint. Using a circular motion, work the paint well into your brush (2a). Then, again using a circular motion, remove the excess paint on a paper towel (2b). If you pass your brush quickly over the palm of your hand, it should seem quite dry (2c).

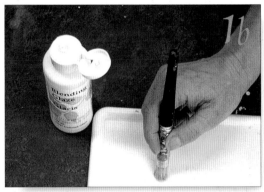

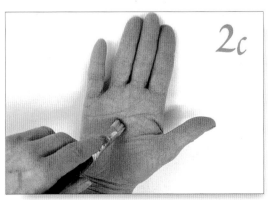

✿ Step 3

Secure your stencil in place with either painter's tape or repositionable stencil adhesive spray. Hold your brush perpendicular to your work and use either a circular or stippling motion to apply your paint (3a). Build up the color gradually to achieve even blending. You can add additional colors if using an overlay (3b). We suggest using a different brush for each color to prevent colors from becoming muddy.

Hint: From time to time you may find that your brush is developing a buildup of paint or is drying out. You can alleviate this problem by swiping your brush across a moist sponge or by working glaze into your brush. Whichever method you use, be sure to remove excess water or glaze from your brush onto a paper towel before you resum stenciling.

SHADING

Often we wish to shade or highlight our roller stenciling. Most of the shading and highlighting of the projects in this book was done with stenciling brushes rather than stenciling rollers. It is easier to achieve controlled shading and highlighting with a brush than with a roller

✿ To add forest green shading to this spring green ivy vine, hold your brush perpendicular to your work and use a circular motion to shade your print. Build up the color gradually. This way you will get even blending.

Frequently we use highlighting and shading to give roundness to an object. To make an object appear round by shading it, position your brush so that it is partially on the stencil and partially on the wall or surface you are stenciling. Using a circular motion, follow around the outside edge of the cutout. This will result in color that is strongest at the outer edge and tapers as it moves toward the center of your object.

shading with a circular motion

To make an object appear round by highlighting, load your stencil brush with a color lighter than the main stencil color in the area to be highlighted. Work the lighter paint into your brush and then un-load most of the paint onto a paper towel. Rub your brush wherever you wish to create a highlight.

too much paint

If paint bleeds under your stencil, you have too much paint on your roller, you are applying too much pressure on the roller, or the roller is too damp. If your prints are too faint, the roller may not have enough paint or you may be applying too little pressure on your roller.

too little paint

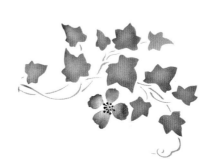

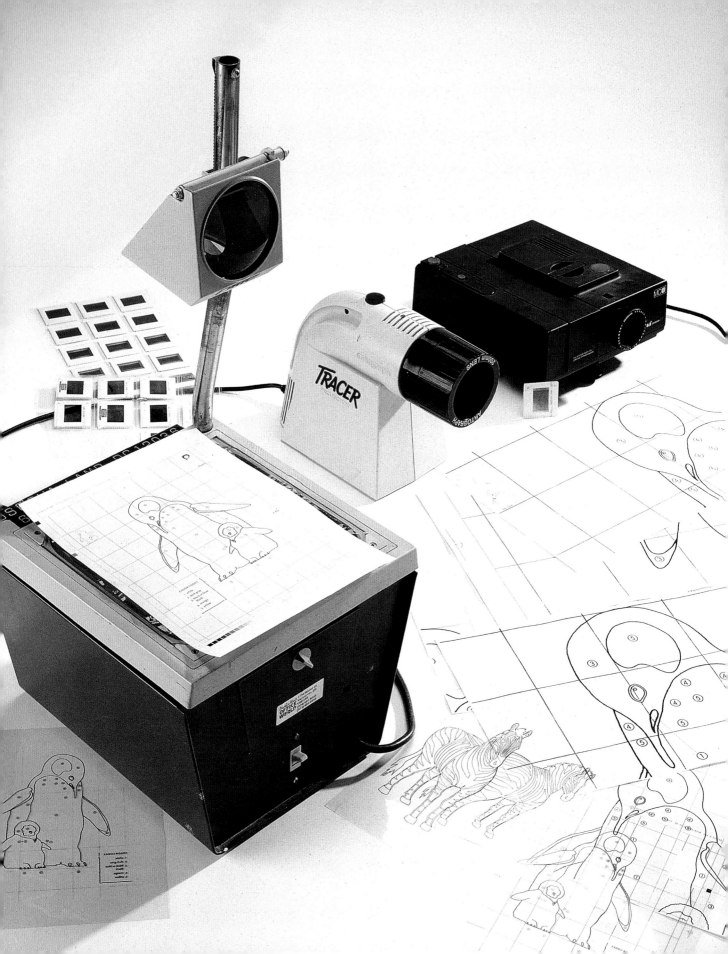

CHAPTER 2

Stenciling Plus

Enlarging & Projecting Stencils

OVERHEAD AND OPAQUE PROJECTOR METHODS

A projector makes it easy to enlarge a design on a wall. The patterns in this book all fit onto an 8½" x 11" page and need to be enlarged many times to become murals. The size of your projected image will depend on how far away from the wall you place the projector. For example, to enlarge an illustration sixfold your projector should be seven or eight feet from the wall. If you find your room too small to get your projector far enough away from the wall to be stenciled, trace your pattern in a larger room and then transfer it to the room you intend to stencil.

A NOTE ABOUT PROJECTORS

It may sound complicated and expensive to use projectors and tracers to make mural stencils, but it becomes more reasonable when you consider that using commercial stencils to create even a modest mural costs several hundred dollars. In that context, renting an overhead projector for a few dollars or even buying an Artograph Tracer for less than a hundred dollars, thus purchasing yourself unlimited stenciling possibilities becomes a bargain.

If you are using an overhead projector, your pattern must be made into a transparency. To transfer a design on paper onto a transparency is easy and inexpensive. Simply photocopy your design onto a piece of clear acetate (available from any office supply store and most photocopy shops for about a dollar). If you are using an opaque projector you can put your line drawing directly on the screen.

FINDING A PROJECTOR

Finding a projector is not difficult. Check with friends, community centers, teachers, or project presenters. Check for rentals in your telephone Yellow Pages under audio/visual, office equipment, and photography shops. We purchased used projectors at a fraction of their original price from an office furniture store.

USING A TRACER PROJECTOR

We produced several of our murals using the small inexpensive Tracer by Artograph®, which we purchased from an art supply store. One of the nice features of the Artograph® is that it does not require transparencies. Because it is an opaque projector it projects the original image. It is helpful to reduce your pattern to the size of the viewer (ours is 5" x 5") because if you have to reposition a large design it can be difficult to align your projection perfectly with the portion of the design you have already traced onto freezer paper. The Tracer enlarges drawings up to twelve times their original size. If we want to enlarge an image more than that, we start with a drawing larger than 5" x 5" and trace a portion at a time. Repositioning artwork in this way is tedious, but it can be done. To use a Tracer, you need a very dark room in which to project your image. The darker the room, the sharper and brighter your image will appear. (See the Resources section for Tracer suppliers.) For small projects the Junior Tracer by Artograph® may be adequate. Its viewer bed is 3" x 3".

USING A SLIDE PROJECTOR

If you own a slide projector or can rent or borrow one, you will find it quite easy to reproduce your "artwork." Use a slide of your image rather than a design on paper or a transparency. As with the overhead and opaque projectors, you will need a wall large enough and a room dark enough to project your image to the desired size. For step-by-step instructions refer to Enlarging an Image Using a Projector.

To make a slide, take a picture of your subject with your camera. Using slide film in your camera (check with your photography store regarding technical questions such as the proper speed of film for shooting indoors or outdoors), take your pictures dead-on to avoid any distortion. Keep a steady hand or use a tripod to ensure a clear picture. Slide images should be simple and contain large, clean blocks of color. Project them directly onto the wall and trace onto freezer paper. *Hint:* During the tracing process you may wish to include the numbered color code on your pattern. Holiday or family slides from long-forgotten times may be waiting for rediscovery in the back of your closet. Dust off the box, sit down with a cup of coffee, and look at them again as possible sources for projection stenciling—your honeymoon spot, that vacation in Hawaii, family pets, old childhood mementos, arty shots taken during college, or silhouttes of your kids at the beach. You just never know!

USING THE SMALL PATTERN

You can easily make the small patterns provided for each project into slides by photocopying them onto acetate and then trimming to fit into a slide holder (available at photography stores).

ENLARGING AN IMAGE USING A PROJECTOR

1. Place your pattern on the bed of your projector or under the viewing area of the Tracer, or place your slide in your slide projector.

2. Turn off the lights in the room and project your image onto the wall. Adjust the projector until your pattern is the size you want and the design is positioned correctly on the wall. Carefully focus until the image is clear. If you are using an overhead, opaque, or Tracer, make the final adjustments to the position of the pattern on the bed of the projector or under the viewing area of the Tracer. Once you are happy with the alignment, tape your pattern in place on the bed of your projector to prevent it from shifting.

3. While still projecting your image, use painter's tape to mark the outer dimensions of your project.

4. Turning the lights back on, cut lengths of freezer paper to cover an area at least a foot longer than the full width and height of the image (one piece of freezer paper may be sufficient). Lay strips of freezer paper on the floor, shiny side down. Making sure the room is well ventilated and the floor is protected with newspaper, spray each strip of paper with repositionable stencil adhesive. You may want to do your spraying outdoors. Let the freezer paper sit for a few minutes before applying it to your wall.

5. Turn out the lights again and check to make sure that your projected image is still straight and sharply focused. Now stick the freezer paper to the wall where the projected image appears and smooth out as many wrinkles as possible, using your hands. We have found that the easiest way to do this is to apply one sheet of paper at a time, as you would wallpaper. Hold the paper vertically, slightly away from the wall. Stick the freezer paper on the wall, working from top to bottom. Once you have the first sheet in place, align the second, and continue in this fashion until you have covered the entire area on which the image appears. Use painter's tape around the top, bottom, and sides of the freezer paper to ensure the paper doesn't shift. Make sure you use painter's tape rather than masking tape, because masking tape may remove paint from the wall when it is removed. Use clear packing tape to cover the seams where the sheets of paper meet.

6. Use a fine tip permanent marker to trace the projected image onto the sheet of paper. It is important to use a permanent felt marker; otherwise, your pen color will bleed into your paint. Proceed slowly with the tracing and make sure to mark all the lines. To prevent smudges, start at the right side and move left if you are right-handed and vice versa if you are left-handed. Leslie and I joke that we picked each other as best friends because one of us is left-handed and one is right-handed and so we can both trace at the same time.

ENLARGING WITHOUT A PROJECTOR

THREE GRID SYSTEMS

If you can't find a projector, the next easiest way to transfer your artwork from a small to a large format is to use a grid system. No special artistic talent is required, just accurate copying.

Freehand Grid Drawing
METHOD

1. Photocopy and enlarge the grid below onto a transparency.

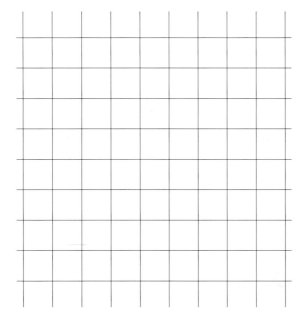

2. Place the transparent grid so that it covers your pattern.
3. Determine the size you want your mural to be. For instance, if you want to double the size, 1" on your drawing would be 2" on the wall. To make the design twelve times larger, 1" on the drawing would be 12" on the wall.

4. Once you have determined the size of the mural, cut and tape sheets of freezer paper the size of the area to be stenciled, plus a one-foot allowance on both sides.
5. Spray the back of the freezer paper (the matte side) with repositionable adhesive. Let it dry for a few minutes.
6. Stick the freezer paper to the wall, one sheet at a time, wallpapering style. Tape the seams with clear packing tape or painter's tape. Use painter's tape around the outside of the freezer paper to ensure that it stays in place.
7. Draw the grid lines on the shiny side of the freezer paper using a permanent felt marker. Use one color of marker to draw your grid, and a different color marker to draw your design. This way you will avoid confusion when the lines cross or are close together.
8. Now simply transfer the art from each square on the small line drawing to the corresponding square on the wall. Step back occasionally to check the overall effect and smooth out any uneven or jerky lines.
9. When all the squares are completed, refer to the step-by-step instructions for the particular mural you are working on.

Photocopying with a Grid

If you are one of those who hates to draw anything freehand, don't despair. Let your photocopier be your projector. Notice that each pattern has a grid pattern laid in behind. This will be your guide for recreating the pattern in a larger size. First, photocopy the pattern from this book at 200%. Then assign each square of the enlarged pattern a letter, printed in the corner of each grid box. The letters will help you put the pattern back together. Then, moving the pattern around the photocopier, enlarge sections of the pattern until it is the final size you desire. This process works best with simple designs. Remember to make sure each piece is enlarged equally. Piece together the enlarged pattern (the pieces of paper will overlap) and tape them together, making sure the grid lines are aligned. Spray the back of the assembled, pieced-together patterns with spray adhesive, and affix it to freezer paper that has been stuck to the wall, glossy side out. Enlarging a pattern this way will take a bit of practice with the photocopy machine. Don't hesitate to ask the people at the service bureau if you need help.

Enlarging a Pattern on a Computer

If you have access to a computer and scanner, you can enlarge your patterns on the computer and print them out on your printer. This method works best with drawing or desktop publishing programs such as Corel Draw, Adobe Pagemaker, Quark Xpress or Microsoft Front Page. Scan the pattern as a bitmapped image, import the image into your program, and print the image at the enlargement percentage that you would like. Set your program to tile the image as your final size will likely be much larger then the maximum single page size of your printer. Match up the grids on each pattern piece and follow the assembly instructions above for *Photocopying with a Grid*.

CREATING YOUR OWN STENCILS FROM PHOTOS, SLIDES, OR CLIP ART

We warned you in the Introduction that potential stencils lurk everywhere, and we were not kidding. When our editor, Susan, showed us a photo of her new puppy, Frank, my first thoughts were not, "Oh, what an adorable puppy!" but rather, "He'd make a great stencil!"

Pictures with clean lines and solid blocks of color are ideal for creating stencils. Take a look at Frank. Notice the clearly defined blocks of color (I'm sure that's what Susan had in mind when she selected him).

Let's take a look at the step-by-step process of creating wall art from the photo of Frank.

First, I had a transparency made from the photo so I could project the image with my overhead projector onto freezer paper. I could just as easily have used my Tracer Projector by Artograph® or any opaque projector, in which case I would not have needed to make a transparency. If I had had a slide rather than a photo, I could have simply projected the slide with a slide projector.

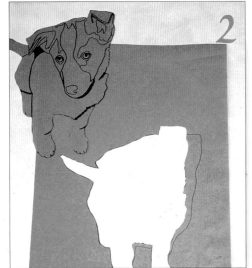

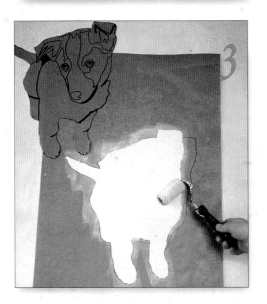

❀ Once I had the puppy projected to the desired size on the wall, I traced around the outside of his body, outlined blocks of color on the freezer paper, and coded the outlined blocks white, brown, dark brown, gray, pink, black, blue, and shadow.

❀ Next I cut along the outline of the puppy's body and removed the cutout. I roller stenciled the puppy's body white and shaded around the outside edge with gray paint to define the body's shape and to provide the illusion of roundness. If you are stenciling white onto a white background it is especially important to shade with gray; otherwise, your image won't show up against the wall.

❀ Once the paint was dry (with the help of a hairdryer), I repositioned the cutout and continued stenciling, one color at a time, replacing cutouts when necessary, until the puppy was painted. To put the sparkle in Frank's eyes, I created a tiny stencil, using a piece of painter's tape punched with a hole punch.

Even the Monalisa can be Stenciled!

Projecting Standard Stencils

*I*t doesn't get any easier than this. Take one of your existing stencils, place it onto the bed of your overhead projector, and project the image to the desired size.

CAVE ART AT THE BAY, VANCOUVER DOWNTOWN, 674 GRANVILLE ST. AT GEORGIA, FURNITURE DEPARTMENT, 6TH FLOOR CANADAS STORE, CANADAS STYLE SINCE 1670

Our friend and colleague, Georgina King, used a projected standard stencil to great effect. She used Buckingham's Cave Art Motif Stencil as a projection stencil in a cave art frieze featured as a backdrop for a furniture setting on the floor of The Bay department store. First, Georgina color-washed the wall a golden hue. The definition for the frieze was created by painting along and between two sheets of torn freezer paper (see photo).

The freezer paper was torn in an irregular fashion, sprayed with stencil adhesive, and positioned onto the wall to act as guide-lines for the frieze. The area between the sheets of paper was roller stenciled with shadow glaze, and the edgesof the frieze were further defined by brush stenciling with black and brown along the torn edge of the paper. The freezer paper was then removed and the cave art figures were projected, traced onto freezer paper, and arranged along the frieze for cutting and stenciling. The figures were stenciled using an array of colors, including yellow, terra-cotta, brown, red, and black. (For a step-by-step discussion of the cave art stencils, see page 56)

CHAPTER 3

How to Use this Book

TOOLS AND MATERIALS

The basic tools and materials you will need for each project are:

- Freezer paper
- Painter's or low-tack tape
- Repositionable stencil spray adhesive
- X-acto® or snap-off utility knife
- Black permanent felt marker (fine tip)
- Permanent fine tip felt marker in contrasting color if using the grid system
- Stenciling rollers
- Stencil brushes
- Paint palette
- Spreader
- Paper towels
- Hairdryer (optional, but will speed up drying time)
- Low-luster water-based house paint, Buckingham Roller Stencil Paint, or craft acrylic paint (with glaze or extender as discussed on page 23-24). Each project will list the colors needed and any special tools or materials you will require.

Some projects require "shadow glaze." This is a mix of one part raw umber water-based paint to four parts glaze.

PROJECTING AND TRACING

For each project, you will need enough freezer paper to cover the area you want to stencil. The freezer paper should be sprayed with repositionable adhesive spray and affixed firmly to the wall. Then you will need to project the image onto the paper, using whichever projection technique you choose, and trace the pattern using a fine tip felt pen.

A NOTE ABOUT CUTTING

One of the most important tools in projection stenciling is a cutting knife with a sharp blade. *It is essential to replace your blade frequently so you are always working with a sharp blade*. We prefer X-acto® blades or utility knives with snap-off blades with an acute angle, similar to the X-acto® blades. To save on the cost of replacement blades, we sharpened our X-acto® blades with a sharpening stone. A sharp new blade is just a snap away for utility knives, as refills are inexpensive.

One of the major differences between traditional stenciling and projection stenciling is that in projection stenciling you cut out your stencil right on the surface you are stenciling. Your cutting technique will vary depending on the surface you are stenciling. If you are stenciling on drywall (or sheetrock), you will want to use a light touch with the knife in order not to score the wall too deeply. Some scoring is not a problem. When it comes time to repaint, a light sanding will make shallow score lines disappear. If you wish to avoid any scoring, use a finger to lift the freezer paper slightly off the surface as you cut along the pattern lines (keeping your finger well out of the way of the blade's progress). If you are cutting on a blind (as in the Merlin project on page 126) you must lift the paper as you cut because it is very easy to cut through the fabric of the blind. When cutting on glass you can use as much or as little pressure as you wish because you can't mark the glass. When stenciling faux inlaid wood you will want to score deeply as the cut line adds to the illusion of inlay.

THE IMPORTANCE OF THE SAMPLE BOARD: A CAUTIONARY TALE

Not long ago I decided to faux finish my living room in rich golden hues. I painted up a few sample boards and they didn't look quite right but I was sure that I could make slight modifications in my color mix and get the desired result. So without testing these "slight modifications" on a sample board, the entire room was basecoated. Well, no matter what glazes I applied, I failed to get an attractive finish, so the whole room had to be basecoated once again. Now, you would think that by this time I would be smart enough to test the basecoat color with the intended glazes, but no. I am a very slow learner. And it gets worse. The room had to be basecoated from stem to stern four times before I was satisfied with the color. Luckily my daughter, Dana, was an apprentice painter at the time and was eager to make some money so I hired her to do the basecoating. However, after painting the room four times, she was barely speaking to me. How much easier it would have been to get the color mix right on a small sample board first! The moral of the story is to test your color blends on a sample board before you begin to paint.

PREPARING YOUR WALL

If you intend to add a fresh coat of paint to your room before undertaking your stenciling project, make sure to allow at least 24 hours drying time before you begin to stencil.

C O L O R G U I D E

■ BLACK		■ DARK BROWN	
□ WHITE		PALE PINK	
METALLIC GOLD		PINK	
■ METALLIC SILVER		DARK PINK	
BONE WHITE		BURGANDY	
LIGHT GRAY		LIGHT RED	
MEDIUM GRAY/GRAY		■ PRIMARY RED/RED	
■ DARK GRAY		■ DEEP RED	
CANARY YELLOW		SOFT LILAC/LIGHT PURPLE	
YELLOW/BRIGHT YELLOW		GREY-PURPLE	
GOLDEN YELLOW		MAUVE	
DARK YELLOW		PURPLE/MEDIUM PURPLE	
OCHRE/YELLOW-OXIDE/DARK GOLD		■ DARK PURPLE	
LIGHT TERRA-COTTA		PERIWINKLE	
GOLDEN TERRA-COTTA		DARK PERIWINKLE	
TERRA-COTTA		SKY BLUE/LIGHT BLUE	
■ DARK TERRA-COTTA/RED BROWN		BLUE/MEDIUM BLUE	
GOLDEN ORANGE		■ DARK BLUE/LIGHT MIDNIGHT BLUE	
ORANGE		■ MIDNIGHT BLUE/BLUE BLACK	
ORANGE RED/RUST		COBALT BLUE	
■ ORANGE BLACK		LIGHT CYAN BLUE/TURQUOISE	
RAW UMBER		CYANO BLUE	
CORAL/SALMON		DARK CYANO BLUE/DARK TURQUOISE	
CLAY RED		LIGHT GREEN	
LIGHT FLESH TONE		SPRING GREEN	
DARK FLESH TONE		PRIMARY GREEN	
LIGHT TAN/LIGHT BEIGE		MEDIUM/BLUE/MOUNTAIN GREEN	
DARK TAN/DARK BEIGE		FOREST GREEN/DARK GREEN	
SOFT BROWN		■ GREEN BLACK	
BROWN			

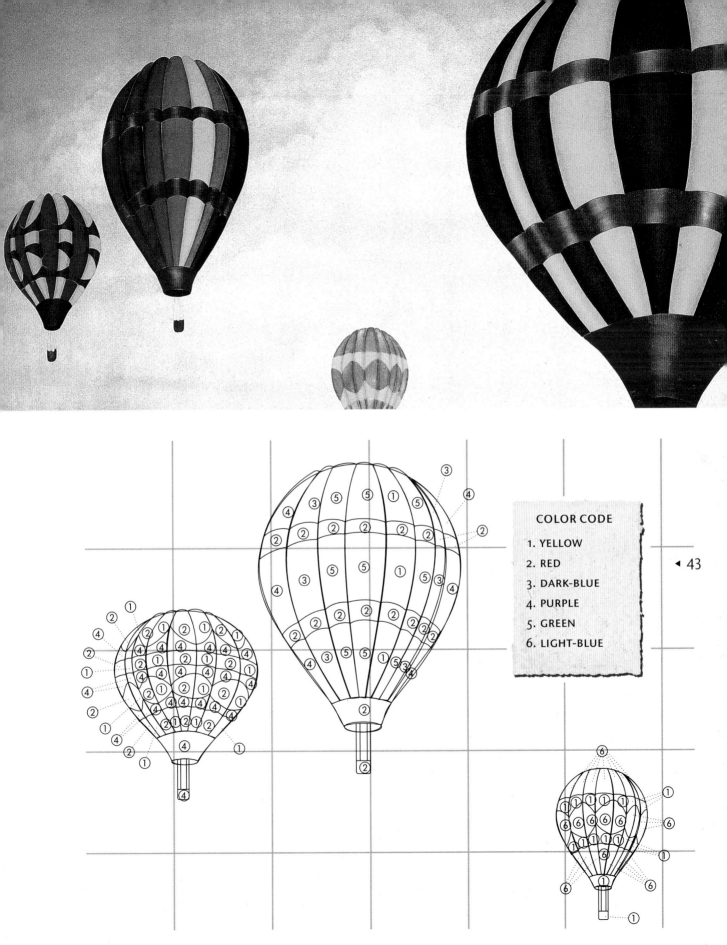

COLOR CODE

1. YELLOW
2. RED
3. DARK-BLUE
4. PURPLE
5. GREEN
6. LIGHT-BLUE

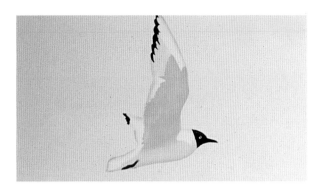

PART II

Sensationally Simple

*Y*our aim may be to stencil large, complex wall murals, but we recommend starting with simpler, less intimidating projects. It is easy to get discouraged if you have a problem with an intricate project. The simple projects outlined in this chapter are ideal for practicing your stenciling techniques and for gaining the confidence to tackle more ambitious projects later. Because the techniques are the same regardless of the size or complexity of the undertaking, you should be able to make the transition from simple to sophisticated without missing a beat.

Zebras

*I*f you don't mind a little company (well, maybe not so little!) in your bathroom, these zebras can give a ho-hum bathroom a playful, exotic ambience.

Willy, my friend's four-year-old, was visiting with his mother when he caught sight of the life-sized zebras in our bathroom. His eyes widened, his jaw dropped, and his body stiffened. His mother rushed to his side to comfort him and to explain that the zebras were merely paintings on the walls. Going down the hall, Willy glanced into the bedroom next door. There, curled up in the middle of the bed, was Leroy, our family cat. The young boy shook his head in disbelief. "Is that cat a painting, too?" he asked.

METHOD

1. Project and trace the zebras onto the freezer paper on the wall as discussed on page 31.
2. Using a sharp X-acto® knife, cut around the main outline of the zebras' bodies. Gently remove this large cutout and set it aside to use later. Run your fingers carefully around the cut edges to make sure they are stuck to the wall.

 47

SPECIAL TOOLS & MATERIALS

- Two stenciling rollers
- Two 1" stencil brushes
- Midnight blue, white, and medium gray paint

See page 40 for details on
STANDARD TOOLS & MATERIALS

3. Roller stencil the zebras' bodies white. Remember to use a "dry" roller stenciling technique as you near the edges of the freezer paper to ensure that the paint does not bleed under the paper. You will need several coats of paint to cover your wall color (you can skip this step if your wall is white). To speed up the drying process, you may wish to use a hairdryer.

4. With a stencil brush and very little paint, shade around the outside edge of the zebras' bodies to define their shape and create the impression of roundness. We used medium gray for shading.

5. Replace the freezer paper cutout of the zebras' bodies so the painted and shaded zebra shapes are completely covered. Tape in place if necessary.

6. Cut out the areas marked midnight blue in your pattern, and roller stencil these areas midnight blue.

7. Using white paint, highlight the chest, belly, and rump as shown in the photograph using a dry brush stenciling technique to add the illusion of roundness.

8. Remove the freezer paper.

9. We stenciled a field of dried ferns at the feet of our zebras and continued around the room, stenciling ferns at the base of the walls. We used the Buckingham Stencils' fern stencil, but you can use any commercial or homemade stencil you desire. The ferns give a sense of continuity to the room, and the color is reminiscent of a savannah. You can also add ambiance to your room by using one of the popular animal skin patterns, such as zebra stripes, leopard spots, or tiger stripes on pillows, curtains, or area carpets to accent your zebras.

Zebras

① ....

② ....

◄ 51

COLOR CODES

1. MIDNIGHT BLUE
2. WHITE

Wrought Iron Headboard

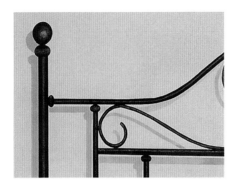

S This wrought iron headboard is the project that led us down the garden path to projection stenciling. Of all the stenciled projects in this book, this is the one with which we have had the most fun. When I tell people the bed is stenciled, they don't understand and start looking at the duvet cover to see if the fabric is stenciled. When I explain that the headboard is painted on the wall, they need to touch it because the illusion is so real. But the best response came when Leslie moved. The moving men tried to pick up her stenciled headboard not once, but three times!

METHOD

1. Mark the height and width of the head of your bed against the wall with pieces of painter's tape. Then move the bed away from the wall. Project the design onto the wall using the painter's tape as your size guideline. Once you have determined the correct size, cover this area with freezer paper and begin tracing your design. Be careful about the placing of the stenciled headboard because you won't be able to move it when it is finished! Use one color of permanent marker for the pattern lines of the headboard (we used black) and another color for the pattern lines of the shadows (we used red).

SPECIAL TOOLS & MATERIALS

- Two stenciling rollers
- ¼" stencil brush
- Blue-black (one part blue, three parts black) or green-black (one part green, three parts black) paint
- White paint
- Shadow glaze (see page 23)

See page 40 for details on
STANDARD TOOLS & MATERIALS

2. Using a sharp X-acto® knife, cut along all pattern lines for the headboard and shadows, except for the base of each vertical bar (see figure below). Remove all pieces that belong to the headboard (the black sections of the pattern), leaving the shadow sections affixed to the wall. Save all the peeled back pieces because you will need them later. (See drawing of peeled back pattern below.) Run your finger around the cut edge of the freezer paper to ensure the edge is securely affixed to the wall.

3. Roller stencil all the "black" sections with blue-black (one part blue, three parts black) or green-black (one part green, three parts black) paint. You will require several coats to get the depth of color you need.

4. Let the black paint dry to touch. You may wish to speed the drying process by using a hairdryer. We recommend using the dryer on medium heat about 18" from the wall.

5. Replace all cutouts, taping if necessary to hold in place.

6. Remove the shadow sections of the headboard and roller stencil using shadow glaze. Let dry.

7. Remove all the freezer paper.

8. Add white highlights to the bars using a ¼" stencil brush and a very dry stenciling technique. Work the white paint into your brush and then unload most of your paint on a paper towel. Rub your brush along the middle of the bars and in the center of the balls. Your white paint should leave a chalk-like appearance. See photo for placement of highlights.

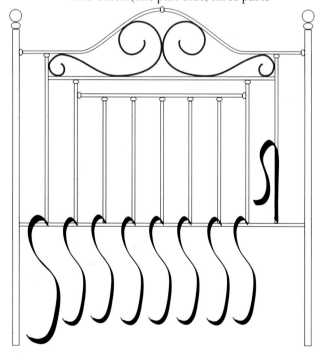

COLOR CODES

1. BLUE-BLACK OR GREEEN-BLACK
2. SHADOW GLAZE.

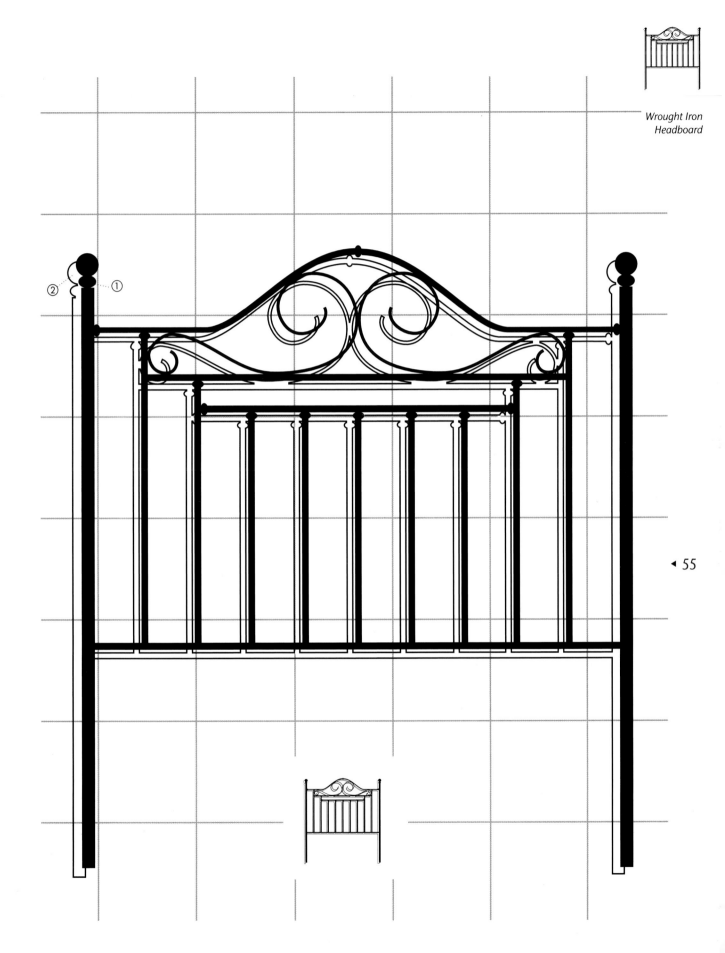

Wrought Iron
Headboard

① ②

◄ 55

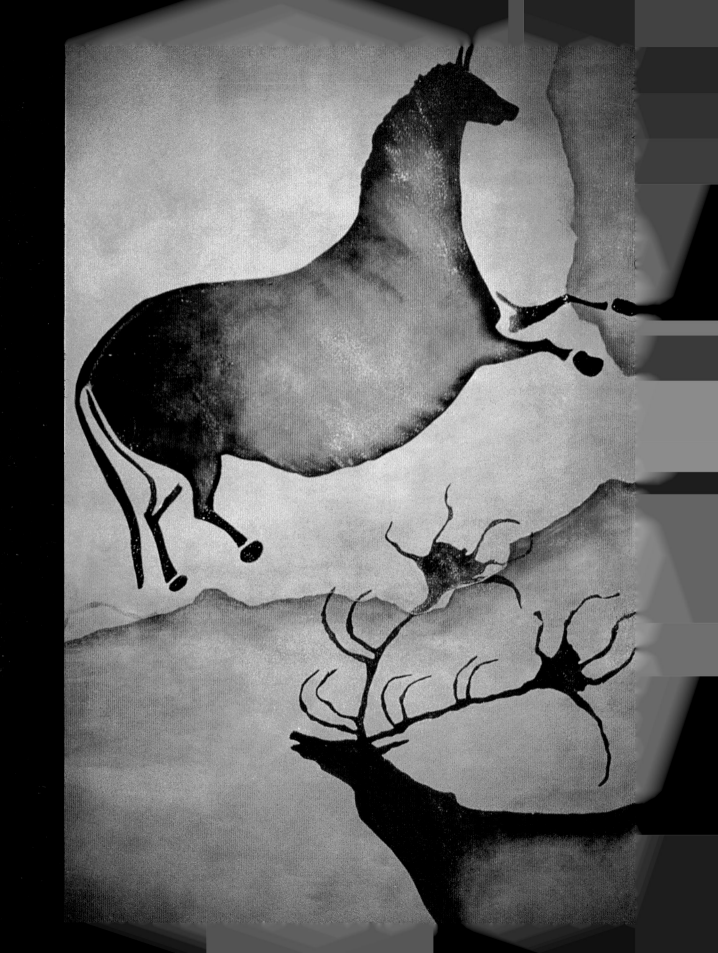

PROJECT 3

Cave Art

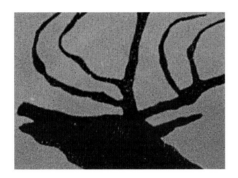

S The mural pictured here was inspired by the cave art drawings in Lascaux, France. The Lascaux cave art drawings were painted by nomadic hunter-gatherers between 15,000 and 20,000 years ago, and they are among the world's oldest known painted murals. These murals were painted by skilled artisans who drew the figures using sticks charred by fire. Pigments used to color these drawings were taken from nature, and included hand-ground minerals, plant matter, and blood. (This makes paint look like quite a nice option!)

Fascination with the history and mystery in these caves brought flocks of tourists to Lascaux, but in recent years the famous caves have been closed because the carbon dioxide from the visitors' breath was causing the ancient colors to fade. Nearby a replica cave has been constructed and paintings copied onto its walls for visitors to view.

The line drawings for these figures were taken directly from figures in the Lascaux Caves.

METHOD

1. To achieve the faux finished "cave wall" background pictured here, apply a glaze mixture (one part golden terra-cotta to four parts glaze) with a stencil roller. Roll the glaze mixture in irregular shapes

◄ 57

SPECIAL TOOLS & MATERIALS

- One stenciling roller
- Four 1" stencil brushes
- Golden terra-cotta, yellow, terra-cotta, brown, rust, and black paint
- Glaze
- Cheese Cloth

See page 40 for details on
STANDARD TOOLS & MATERIALS

roughly three feet by three feet and then use a damp cheesecloth to blot and thin the outside edges. Pounce the glazed surface with the cheesecloth, removing more glaze in some places than others. Once you have dappled one area, move to the next and repeat the process. Because the outside edges of the preceding faux finished area have been thinned with the cheesecloth, you can roll fresh glaze adjacent without risking ugly lap lines. Let the glaze dry overnight.

2. To create the "veins" on the "cave wall," tear several long strips of freezer paper, spray the backs of the strips with stencil adhesive, position the strips on the wall, and use the torn edges as a stencil. With a 1" stencil brush rub brown, black, and terra-cotta paint along the torn paper edge to define the veins.

3. Once your background glaze has dried, position freezer paper where you wish to project your cave art figures and trace these images.

4. Cut out the figures and use a combination of glazes and paints to stencil them in. For these we used yellow, terra-cotta, brown, and rust to intermingle and fill out the bodies. Start stenciling with the lighter colors first, and then add in the darker ones. Shade the edges of the figures black.

5. Remove the freezer paper.

6. Step back in time!

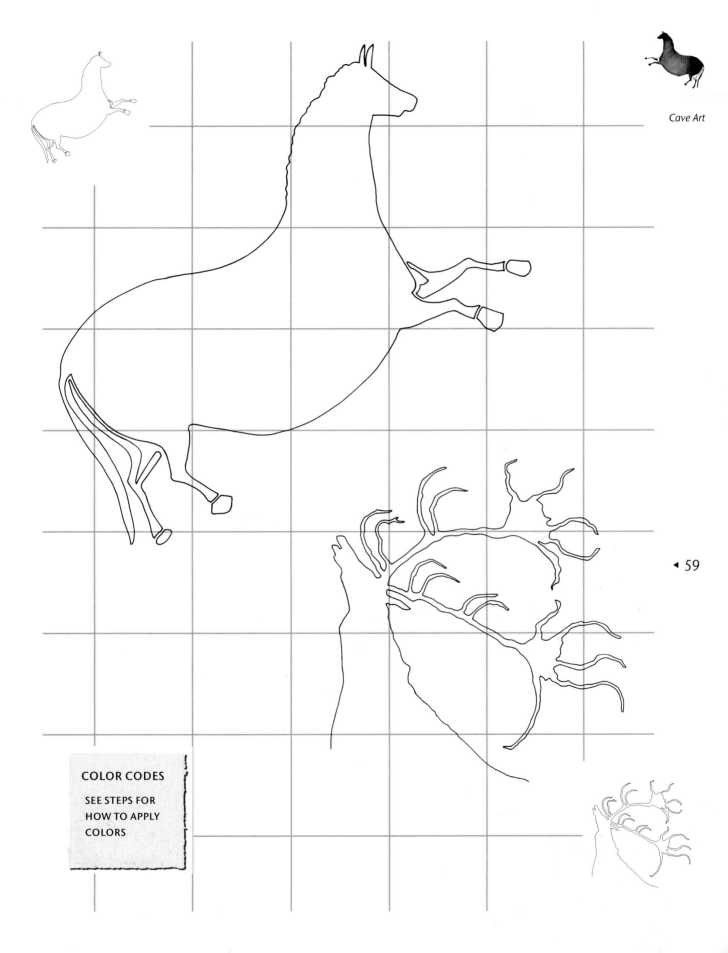

◄ 59

COLOR CODES

SEE STEPS FOR
HOW TO APPLY
COLORS

Penguins

*A*re you tired of the usual bathroom décor of seashells, sea horses, and fish motifs? Be a trendsetter with this pair of penguins leading the way. They will remind you brush your teeth, wash your hands, comb your hair and conserve hot water. Actually they don't say anything, but they do look cool!

METHOD

1. Cut around the outline of the penguins' bodies and remove this large piece. Set it aside to use later.
2. Roller stencil the area white, making sure to use a dry roller technique as you near the edges to prevent the paint from bleeding under the paper. If your wall is a color other than white, you may need several coats of paint to cover it. If your wall is white, you can skip this step.
3. Look at the photograph and shade the penguins' bodies gray around the edges as shown.
4. Once the paint has dried, reposition the large cutout.
5. Cut out the yellow area of the Mama penguin's head and save the cutout.

SPECIAL TOOLS & MATERIALS

- White, gray, black or blue-black, yellow, and orange paint
- One ½" stencil brush
- Two 1" stencil brushes
- Two rollers

See page 40 for details on
STANDARD TOOLS & MATERIALS

6. Cut along the yellow section of the penguin's chest so that you can peel back the freezer paper (don't remove it entirely) to expose the chest area (see the photograph for details).

7. Stencil the exposed part of the penguin's head yellow. Stencil the top part of the chest orange and the rest yellow, blending the colors as you work your way down the chest. Use a very dry brush technique as you stencil the yellow part of the chest so that the yellow fades softly into the white part of the penguin. Reposition this piece.

8. Cut out the Mama penguin's right wing (on the left side of the photograph) and shade it gray where the wing meets the body. Replace the cutout.

9. Cut out the black section around the Mama penguin's other wing and the black around the baby penguin's head. Make sure to leave the white areas of the baby's head, eye, and beak in place on the wall. Roller stencil the exposed areas black.

10. Shade with gray paint around the top of the wing and the top of the baby's head. Replace these cutouts once the paint dries.

11. Cut out around the baby's body. Stencil the baby a mottled gray using a large stencil brush and a pouncing technique (see page 23). Shade around the outside of the baby's body using gray paint. Replace the cutout of the baby's body once the paint below is dry.

12. Cut out all the remaining black sections of the design and roller stencil these areas black. Make sure to leave the white area around the Mama penguin's eye, the eye's white highlight, and beak highlight in place.

13. Cut under the baby's left wing (on the right side of the photograph) and peel back the paper under the wing. Shade this exposed area gray along the edge. Cut out the baby's other wing and shade it gray where the wing meets the body. Cut out around the baby's feet and leave the freezer paper above the feet to shade gray along the top of the feet (see the photograph for direction). Note the little line that separates the Mama's foot from her body. Cut along this little line and shade it gray.

14. Remove all the freezer paper and stand back to enjoy the chill!

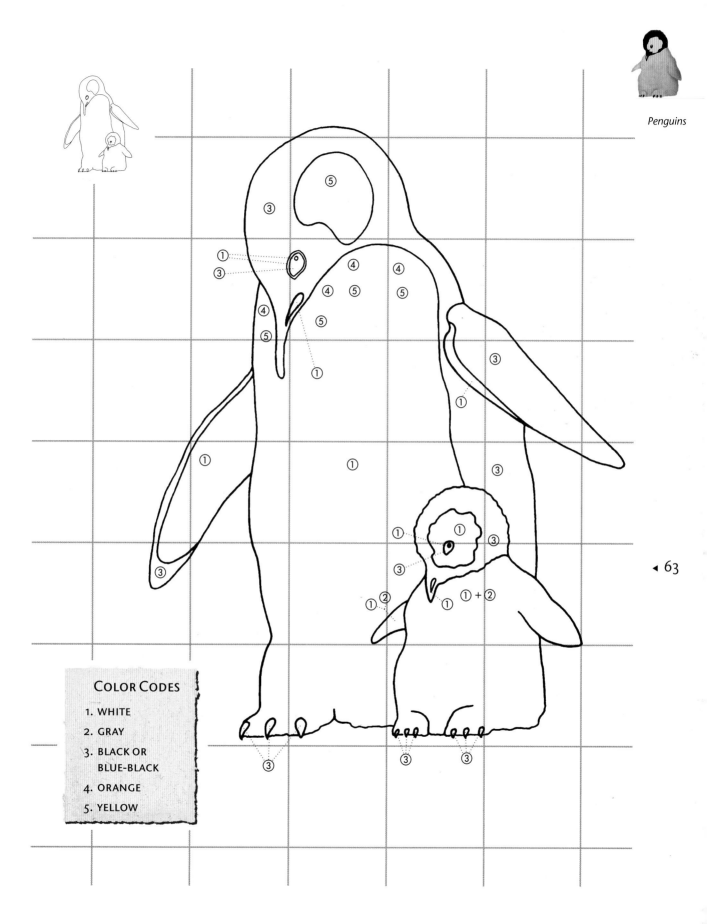

◄ 63

COLOR CODES

1. WHITE
2. GRAY
3. BLACK OR
   BLUE-BLACK
4. ORANGE
5. YELLOW

PROJECT 5

Whales

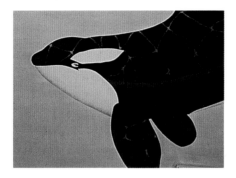

$\mathcal{T}$his mural is great for a kid's room, but adults love it too. We painted this mural in my parents' guest room and they love it. The only problem is my stepdad says he feels like he has to put on scuba gear before he enters.

METHOD

1. To prepare your wall, basecoat it with low-luster, very light sky blue latex paint.

2. Using a sharp X-acto® knife, cut out the water portion of the pattern by cutting along the waterline and the underside of the top whale. Remove the cutout and save it to use later.

3. To give the water a translucent look, roll on a thin layer of water-based glaze (mixed four parts glaze to one part light blue paint). Work quickly to avoid lap lines. If you wish, you may paint your sea rather than glaze it. If you want to use paint for the water, choose a color that is slightly darker than your wall color.

4. Using a stencil brush, shade the waterline a slightly darker blue.

5. If you used glaze for the sea, take a break at this point to allow it to dry. Remember that glazes take quite a bit longer than paints to dry. You can speed up this process by using a hairdryer.

6. Once the sea is dry, replace its cutout.

SPECIAL TOOLS & MATERIALS

- Three stenciling rollers (or one roller and two refills
- Three 1" stencil brushes
- Two ½" stencil brushes
- White, black, blue-black, light blue, dark blue, light gray, and gray paint

See page 40 for details on

STANDARD TOOLS & MATERIALS

7. Cut around the outside of the bodies of the whales. Remove the cutouts and save to use later.

8. Using a roller and white paint, roller stencil the whales' bodies. You may require several coats of paint to achieve good coverage.

9. When the paint is dry, use a stencil brush to rub light gray paint around the edges of the whales' bodies to give a three-dimensional effect.

10. When the light gray paint dries, replace the whale's bodies back into their original positions, making sure the fit is perfect.

11. Cut around the outside edge of the whales' eyes, including both the black and whites of the eyes.

12. Cut out the tiny black part of the eye, remove it, and stencil the opening black using a small stencil brush.

13. Replace the eye cutout once the black paint is dry.

14. Cut out the blue-black parts of the whales, being careful to leave the eyes affixed to the wall. Roller stencil these areas blue-black. Several coats may be necessary to achieve even coverage.

15. Highlight the whales' bodies with white paint using a very dry brush technique. See the photo for where to place the highlights.

16. Cut along the water line on the top whale. Remove the whales's lower body and use a dry brush technique to define the water lines.

17. Cut out the seagull in the foreground and roller stencil it white, setting the cutout aside to use later. Let the paint dry.

18. Using a stencil brush, shade the underbody of the bird light gray.

19. Reposition the seagull cutout.

20. Cut out the distant wing and roller stencil the exposed area light gray.

21. Replace the distant wing cutout.

22. Cut out the gray part of the forward wing and stencil it gray.

23. Cut out the black sections of the seagull and stencil them black.

24. Use the wooden end of an artist's brush dipped in white paint to dot in the seagull's eye.

25. Cut out the silhouettes of the distant birds and stencil them light gray.

26. Remove all the freezer paper.

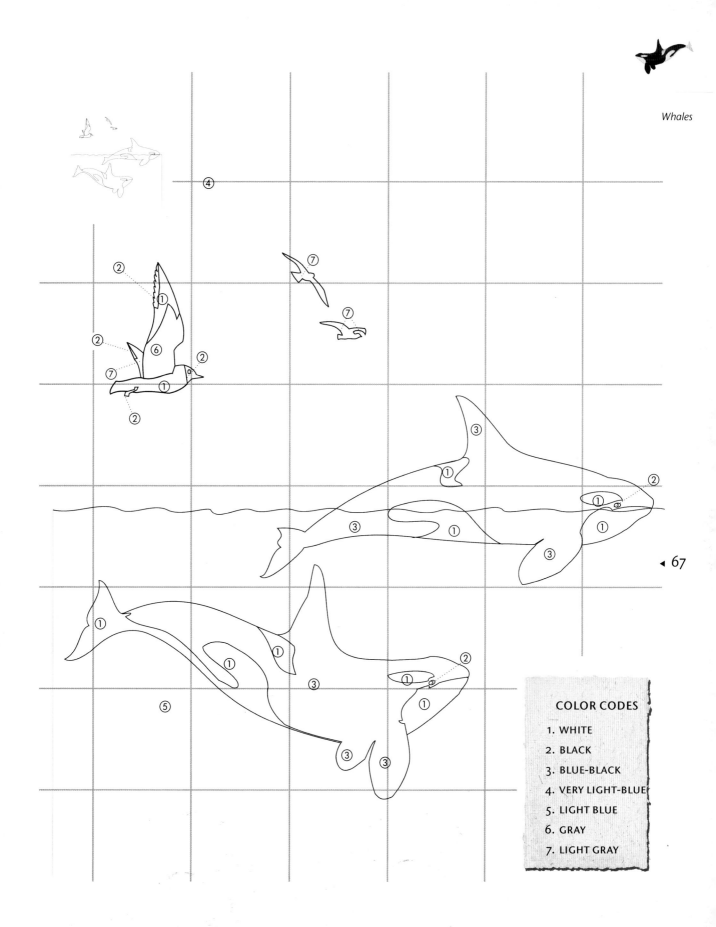

◄ 67

COLOR CODES

1. WHITE
2. BLACK
3. BLUE-BLACK
4. VERY LIGHT-BLUE
5. LIGHT BLUE
6. GRAY
7. LIGHT GRAY

A Fishy Story

I painted this porthole scene to hang in my husband's home office. He is the nutritionist for a fish food company and I thought that if his boss checked up on him it would look good if Greg appeared submerged in his work.

This mural was painted on a piece of hardboard so it is completely portable. If you are renting, or move often, you may wish to consider stenciling your work of art onto a portable surface. This works very well for faux window scenes. You can change your window views as the season changes.

METHOD

1. Basecoat the hardboard with low-luster white latex paint and allow it to dry overnight before affixing your freezer paper pattern. Do not use flat paint.

2. With your felt marker, mark any spot where the border ring (which represents the bronze casing of the porthole) meets the port opening. This mark will be used as registration for accurate repositioning of this cutout.

3. Cut out the border ring and save the cutout.

4. Roller stencil the casing with Blonde Bronze Base Metallic Surfacer. Apply several coats, allowing the paint to dry between coats. Use a hairdryer to speed up the drying process.

5. While the final coat of Blonde Bronze Base is still slightly wet or

SPECIAL TOOLS & MATERIALS

- Two stenciling rollers
- One disposable foam brush
- Fantail paint brush
- An assortment of stencil brushes
- Blonde Bronze Base Metallic Surfacer
- Patina Blue Antiquing Solution
- Glaze
- Light blue, blue, purple, pink, burgundy, yellow, black, white, gold, and silver paint

See page 40 for details on
STANDARD TOOLS & MATERIALS

tacky, apply Patina Blue Antiquing Solution with a disposable brush. Allow to fully air dry. Additional coats of Patina may be applied to achieve the desired color.

6. Once the Patina Blue is dry, reposition the ring cutout.

7. Cut out the screws and stencil them gold. Save one of these circular cutouts. Shade around the outside of the screws with dark gold (mix black into the gold).

8. Take the circular cutout you saved, and follow your line drawing to cut out the cross in its center. Use this circular cutout as a stencil to paint the slots in the screws. Use a stencil brush and a paint mixture that is half gold and half black.

9. Remove the freezer paper covering the porthole opening.

10. With a stencil roller apply a thin layer of light blue glaze (one part light blue paint, four parts glaze). Allow the glaze to dry. Glazes dry more slowly than paints, so you may want to take a break at this point. You can speed up the drying time by using a hairdryer.

11. Reposition the opening cutout using the mark you made in step two for registration.

12. Cut out around the outside of the salmons' bodies and remove these pieces.

13. Roller stencil these openings white.

14. For the salmon that have a white midline, replace their cutouts, and cut around the midline. Remove the cutouts, but leave the paper midline attached to your board to act as a mask.

15. Once the white paint dries, use stencil brushes to stencil bands of color. I used

purple, blue, pink, and yellow and blended one color into the next. Stencil a little darker around the outside edges of the fish to give them some roundness. Allow the paint to dry.

16. Replace the salmon cutouts. Cut out the tails and the fins, and with a stencil brush add a little color to them for definition. Dip a fantail paint brush into a little dark paint, and drag the brush through the tails and some of the fins to produce a dark streaking.

17. Cut along the open end of the operculums (or gill coverings. At last my biology degree has come in handy!). Flip these up and stencil along the cut edge. I used burgundy.

18. Cut out the pieces representing the mouth and stencil these openings. I used purple and pink.

19. Cut out around the whites of the eyes. Remove these cutouts and stencil the eyes white.

20. Dip the tip of a stencil brush handle into black paint and dab a black circle in the white on each eye. Once the black dries, use the handle of a small paint brush to similarly add a speck of white to the black on each eye.

21. Remove the fish cutouts. Add shimmer to the fishes' bodies by using a large stencil brush and a dry brush technique to rub a little silver paint over their entire bodies.

22. Remove all freezer paper.

23. With a stencil brush and gold paint add highlights to the bronze casing. I added highlights on the top left and bottom right (inside of the casing).

LIMITING YOUR SCOPE

*T*here are many reasons why it may be a good idea to limit the scope of your mural to a confined area. A composition of limited scope can find a home in almost any room as opposed to a mural that fills an entire wall. Also, painting a mural that covers the entire wall creates the dilemma of how to incorporate the remaining three walls. But a mural painted within an area with natural boundaries such as a door, tabletop, or recessed area in a wall or artificial boundaries (such as a stencilled door, window, or archway) avoids this problem. Also, limited areas will not tax your artistic ability nearly as much as an entire wall because you won't have to deal with the nasty problem of perspective. If we haven't convinced you yet, here's another reason. If you are aiming to paint a convincing trompe l'oeil, it is far easier to carry off the illusion within a confined area than it is over an entire wall.

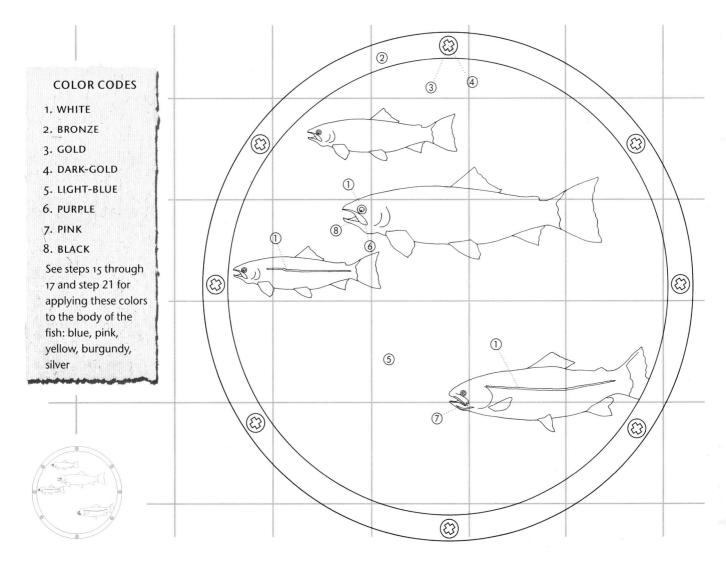

COLOR CODES

1. WHITE
2. BRONZE
3. GOLD
4. DARK-GOLD
5. LIGHT-BLUE
6. PURPLE
7. PINK
8. BLACK

See steps 15 through 17 and step 21 for applying these colors to the body of the fish: blue, pink, yellow, burgundy, silver

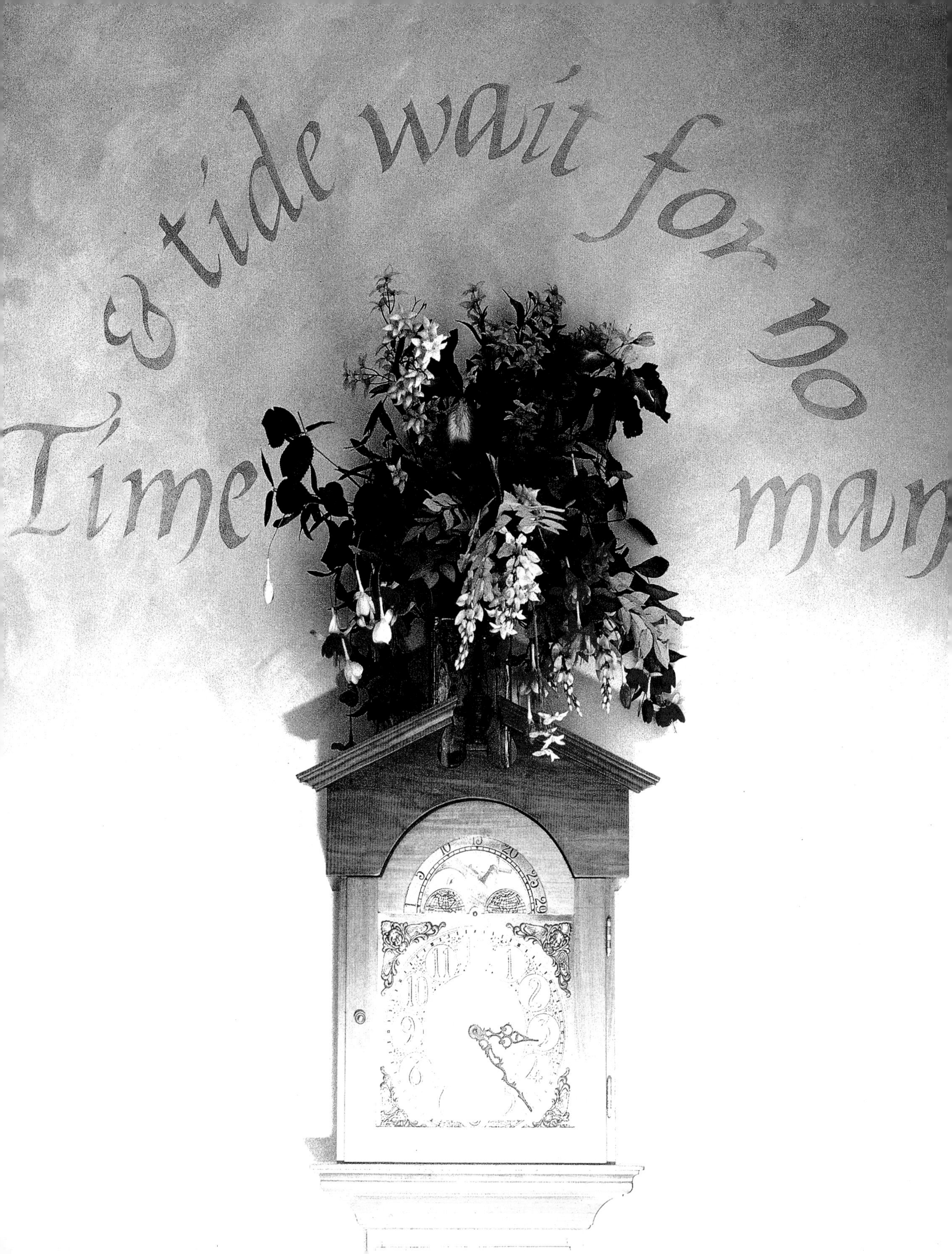
Time & tide wait for no man

Walls that Talk

Walls present the perfect opportunity to immortalize words of wisdom. There are many things to consider when thinking about what to write on your wall. It is important to choose words that have a special importance to you and fit appropriately into the room. Sometimes, an apt quotation can come to mind out of everyday circumstances. Leslie puzzled over what to "write" on the walls of her home. She pored over books of quotations, poetry, clever sayings in greeting cards, but nothing seemed to fit. Running late, as usual, she missed the ferry again. Glancing over at the grandfather clock in the hallway she said to herself, "Time and tide wait for no man!" That was it. The quote she'd been searching for. She briefly considered putting these words of William Shakespeare above a washing machine in the laundry room as a pun, but decided against it. She reconsidered and stenciled them in the hall above the grandfather clock and now they serve as a constant reminder that time and tide wait for very few women as well.

Different rooms require different types of lettering. Long, flowing scripts are more whimsical than bold, formal "faces." If you are uncertain about the size and style of your lettering, do a quick mockup on paper and tape it in place. This will give you a good feel as to what the final design will look like. Books and computers are great sources of different lettering styles or "fonts." Your own handwriting can also be very effective (Even if ours isn't!).

SPECIAL TOOLS & MATERIALS

- One stencil roller
- Gold paint

See page 40 for details on
STANDARD TOOLS & MATERIALS

Consider a nursery rhyme circling a child's room, or a list of spices and herbs running down a kitchen wall. The options are endless. To achieve a subtle look, use a color that is a tone lighter or darker than your wall color or try using a glossy water-based clearcoat over a wall that has been painted with a flat latex.

METHOD

1. First determine the style of lettering you would like to use. This project uses an italic face. For this style of lettering, type your message onto a computer in a large font size so that it fits on an 8½" x 11" page (and fits on a standard transparency sheet). If you are taking your letters out of a book, enlarge them on a photocopier and then arrange them so they spell out your message. Glue the message onto a sheet of white paper, making sure that the distance between each letter is properly spaced.

Then make a transparency. Note: Varied and unusual patterns are more easily done by formatting them on your computer first.

2. Using repositionable spray adhesive, affix your freezer paper to a wall. (You may want to draw a horizontal line across the area you wish to project your letters onto if they are to be stenciled in a straight line. If you are stenciling the message in a circular or semicircular shape, draw in a guideline to help on the freezer paper.)

3. Once the message has been projected and is in the correct position, trace the letters using a permanent fine tip felt pen.

4. Place the freezer paper on the desired wall or surface to be stenciled. Cut out the letters using an X-acto® knife or a utility knife with a snap-off blade and remove them.

5. Using gold paint, roller stencil the cutout letters. You may need more than one coat. Let the paint dry between coats and remove all the freezer paper. Now the writing really is on the wall!

Note: If you are planning a very detailed project or a message on a hard-to-reach wall, it might be easier to project your image onto canvas or a panel of wood and then mount it.

COLOR CODE

1. GOLD.

A B C D E F G
H I J K L M N O
P Q R S T
U V W X Y Z

a b c d e f g
h i j k l m n o
p q r s t
u v w x y z

Walls That Talk

Giant Poppies

beautiful French-dyed silk scarf designed by the late Joey Haynes was the inspiration for this wall mural. Joey was a talented artist, teacher, and writer and the wife of a good friend of ours. She loved gardening and this passion was often reflected in her artwork.

Keep an open mind when looking for design ideas. Inspiration may appear on scarves, T-shirts, tote bags, or, in fact, just about anywhere. We often carry a small camera with us because you never know when a good idea for a design might walk by.

METHOD

1. The wall for this project was basecoated with a low-luster white latex to make the poppies stand out from their background.

2. Using an X-acto® knife, cut out all the areas indicated as red, including the large border and the flowers. *Note:* Save all the border pieces. All the flower cutouts are a lot of work, but well worth the effort. Stencil these areas red using a stencil roller, being careful to use the dry roller technique as you near the edge of the stencil. Let the paint dry. You will need several coats of paint to get the desired intensity of color. To speed up the drying process, you may wish to use a hairdryer. Replace the border pieces.

SPECIAL TOOLS & MATERIALS

- Three or four stencil rollers (or one roller and three roller refills)
- Two ½", one 1" stencil, and one ⅝" brush
- Deep red, light green, green, black, white, and purple paint

See page 40 for details on
STANDARD TOOLS & MATERIALS

3. With a little bit of purple on a 1" stencil brush, blend purple into the red of the poppy flower, concentrating mainly on the tops and bottoms of the petals.

4. Cut out the black pieces next and discard the cutouts. Roller stencil the large areas that form the black background and the flower centers. It is necessary to change to a ½" stencil brush as you near the edge of the freezer paper to prevent the black paint from overlapping into the red flowers. You will probably need to apply several coats of black to achieve good coverage.

5. Cut out the light green leaves and stems next. Discard the cutouts and paint the cutout areas various shades of green using a ½" and ⅝" stencil brush combination.

6. Remove all the freezer paper.

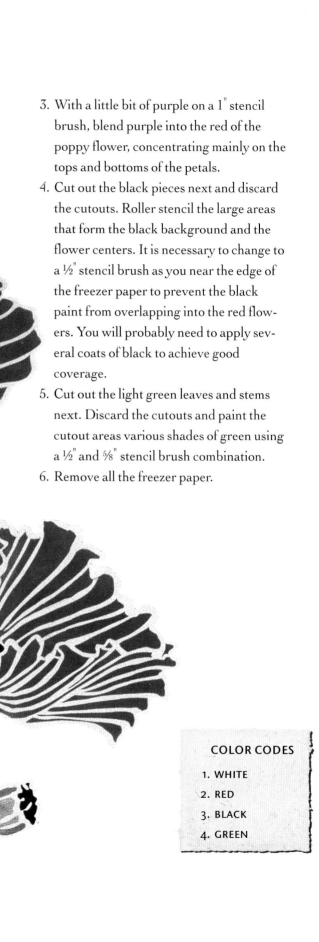

78 ▶

COLOR CODES

1. WHITE
2. RED
3. BLACK
4. GREEN

Giant Poppies

◄ 79

PART III

Kids' Stuff

Children's rooms are the safest and most fun rooms in which to spread our creative wings. They are safe because children are not the harsh critics that many adults are, and fun because our creativity need not have any basis in reality. And here is another consideration. When you announce to your spouse that you are going to stencil your first wall mural, you will probably get a much more favorable response if you say you are undertaking your child's room rather than your living room. However, favorable response has never had much influence on projects we've decided to tackle. We know what our priorities are!

Cow Jumping Over the Moon

W̵alking into this room is like walking into a little piece of heaven where the magic of childhood comes to life. If a cat can play fiddle and a cow can jump over the moon, anything is possible! Soft billowy clouds suspended in an early evening sunset form the backdrop for this nursery rhyme favorite.

METHOD

1. Basecoat your wall with low-luster or semigloss white paint.
2. With painter's tape, tape off the walls adjacent to the mural.
3. The evening sky pictured here was created with sky blue, lilac, and pink latex glazes. To mix the glazes, add one part paint to four parts glaze. The glaze that I used was one that contained an extender. If your glaze does not contain an extender you will need to add one so that you have enough open time to manipulate the glaze before it sets up. Follow the manufacturer's instructions for the brand you are using. We recommend having two people apply the glaze. Using a large (4″) high density foam roller, one person rolls on the glaze, while the other follows behind with an unloaded roller to ensure there is no ugly "overlapping" where one pass of the roller connects with the next pass. It helps to use a second person when you are working with latex glazes because your open time is quite limited. Once you start this process, you don't want to be interrupted, so make sure the kids are fed and the answering machine is on. To achieve the multicolored

sky, roll on a band of blue glaze that comes about a third of the way down the wall.

Then, immediately below the blue, roll on the lilac glaze with a fresh roller. Where the colors meet, roll your roller back and forth many times. This allows the colors to melt into each other so you can't tell where one color ends and the next begins. Directly below the lilac add a band of pink glaze and blend the pink into the lilac the same way you blended the blue into the lilac.

4. Use your largest brush to add soft clouds. Dip your brush in white paint, and remove excess paint by blotting your brush on a paper towel. With a freshly loaded brush, add clouds using a pouncing motion. The foreground clouds are formed when your brush is freshly loaded, and background clouds appear as your brush gets drier.

5. Once your sky has dried, project and trace the cow stencil onto the freezer paper positioned on the wall.

6. Using a sharp X-acto® knife, cut out the moon (cutting around the cow's feet). Carefully remove and save this cutout for later use. Run your fingers carefully around the cut edges to make sure they are affixed to the wall.

7. Roller stencil the moon as evenly as possible, using canary yellow paint. Use a dry roller technique as you near the edges of the freezer paper to prevent paint from bleeding under the paper. You will need more than one coat. With a stencil brush, shade the outer edge of the moon terra-cotta. This shading adds a three-dimensional effect to the stencil. You may want to use a hairdryer to speed up the drying process.

8. When the paint is dry, replace the moon

cutout, taping if necessary to help hold it in place. Cut out the face and remove all sections of freezer paper representing the facial details of the moon.

9. Roller stencil the moon's facial features light terra-cotta.

10. Cut out the cow's entire body. There are four separate pieces—two of the legs, a tail, and the rest of the body. Save all the cutouts.

11. Stencil the cow's body white. You may need several coats of paint to cover the background color of the wall. Shade around the edge of the entire cow with medium gray to define the shape and to provide a sense of roundness. Let the paint dry. Replace all the cow cutouts.

12. Cut out the ribbon and collar pieces. Save the collar. Stencil these sections blue, shading as desired.

13. Cut out the bell pieces and stencil them gold.

14. Cut out the udder, nostril, and inside ear pieces. Save the inside ear cutout. Use a stencil brush to stencil these sections pink.

15. Reposition the collar cutout and inside ear cutout.

16. Cut out the hooves, pads, horns, and iris of the eye. Stencil these sections black. Save the iris cutout. Reposition the iris cutout once the black paint is dry.

17. Cut around the outside of the cow's eye, but leave this piece in place to act as a mask when stenciling the brown patches.

18. Cut out all the spots on the cow. Stencil these sections soft brown, making sure the eye, inside ear, and collar are protected from paint with their cutouts.

19. For the final touch, add a spot of white paint to the iris of the cow's eye.

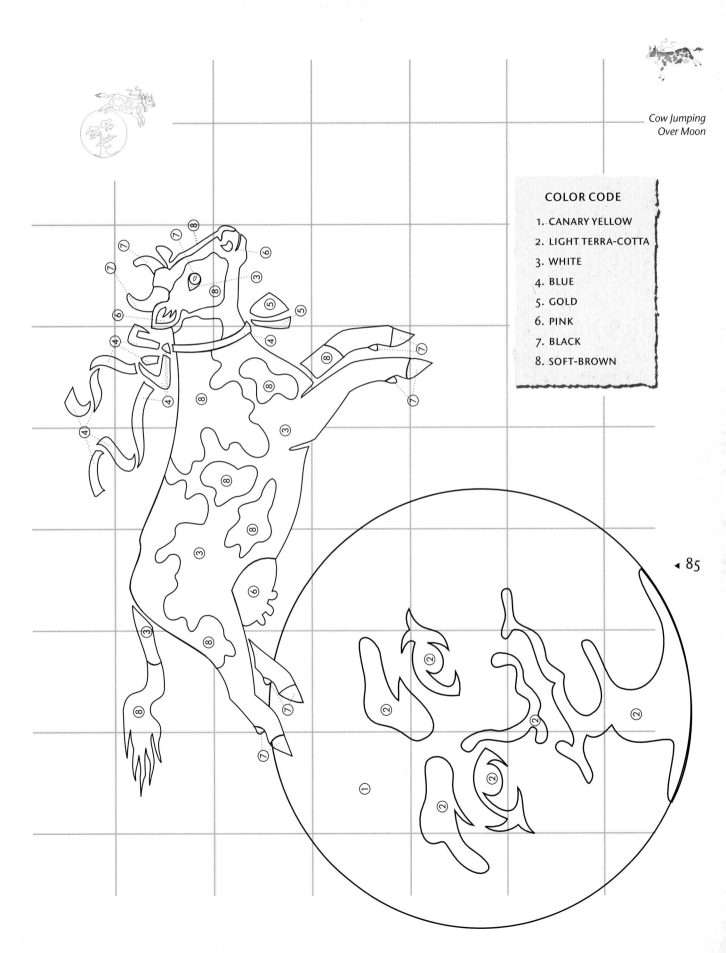

COLOR CODE

1. CANARY YELLOW
2. LIGHT TERRA-COTTA
3. WHITE
4. BLUE
5. GOLD
6. PINK
7. BLACK
8. SOFT-BROWN

◄ 85

Pegasus

*A*quick review of Leslie's and my knowledge of mythology revealed that neither of us had a clue about it. In fact, it was all Greek to us. We racked our brains trying to remember our Grade Seven social studies lessons about the story of Pegasus, the flying horse. "Wasn't he the horse who flew too close to the sun and got his wings burned?" Leslie asked, worried about the appropriateness of this winged horse for a child's room. I replied, "No! That was Icarus!" The only reason I knew that was because friends of mine had a candle company called Icarus and had explained to me the story of the boy who flew too close to the sun. When we finished laughing, we decided that a little more research was necessary.

Leslie was reassured by what we learned. According to Greek mythology, Pegasus was the most noble and beautiful horse ever created. He was a magical creature known for his wisdom and gentleness. He was so pure that he resided on Olympus with the god Zeus. That was good enough for us!

You may wonder what Pegasus is doing for work these days. He's made it big on the silver screen with TriStar Movie Studios!

METHOD

1. To prepare the background, paint a section of the wall to give the impression of a night sky without creating a dark room. Place a large piece of freezer paper on the wall using repositionable spray

◄ 87

SPECIAL TOOLS & MATERIALS

- Two stencil rollers
- An assortment of stencil brushes (¾", ⅝", ½")
- Dark periwinkle, white, pale gray, gold, pink, and black paint

See page 40 for details on
STANDARD TOOLS & MATERIALS

adhesive. Draw a wavy line on the freezer paper with a marker. Cut all the way along the wavy line with an X-acto® knife and remove the cutout. Paint this large area dark periwinkle using a standard roller until you near the edge of the freezer paper. At that point, switch to a stenciling roller and use very little paint to ensure the paint doesn't bleed under the freezer paper. Let this base coat dry.

2. Project the image onto the freezer paper. Position Pegasus at an angle as though taking flight in the middle of the sky. Cut around all of Pegasus' body pieces. Gently remove these cutouts and set it aside to use later. Run your fingers carefully around the cut edges of the freezer paper to make sure they are stuck to the wall.

3. Roller stencil Pegasus' body white. You will require several coats of paint to achieve good coverage. Be sure to allow time for each coat to dry. You may wish to use a hairdryer to speed up drying time. Hold the dryer about 18" from the wall on a low setting.

4. When the paint is dry, use a stencil brush to rub pale gray paint around the edge of Pegasus' body to give a three-dimensional effect.

5. When the shading is dry, reposition Pegasus' body back into its original place, making sure the fit is perfect.

6. Cut out the pieces indicated as gold, including the mane, tail, hooves, and wings. Stencil them in gold.

7. Next, cut out the shadow insets in the body and legs and discard the cutouts. Stencil these areas pale gray.

8. Cut out the nostril and inner ear and discard cutouts. Stencil these two spaces pink.

9. Cut out the eye and stencil it black. Save the cutout.

10. Reposition the eye cutout. Cut out the highlight and stencil it white.

11. Remove the freezer paper.

12. We stenciled stars all over the background and have included two stencils for you to enlarge and use. Place them randomly over the night sky in gold or silver. You can carry the starry night theme further by stenciling stars onto pillow cases, sheets, furniture, curtains, and lampshades.

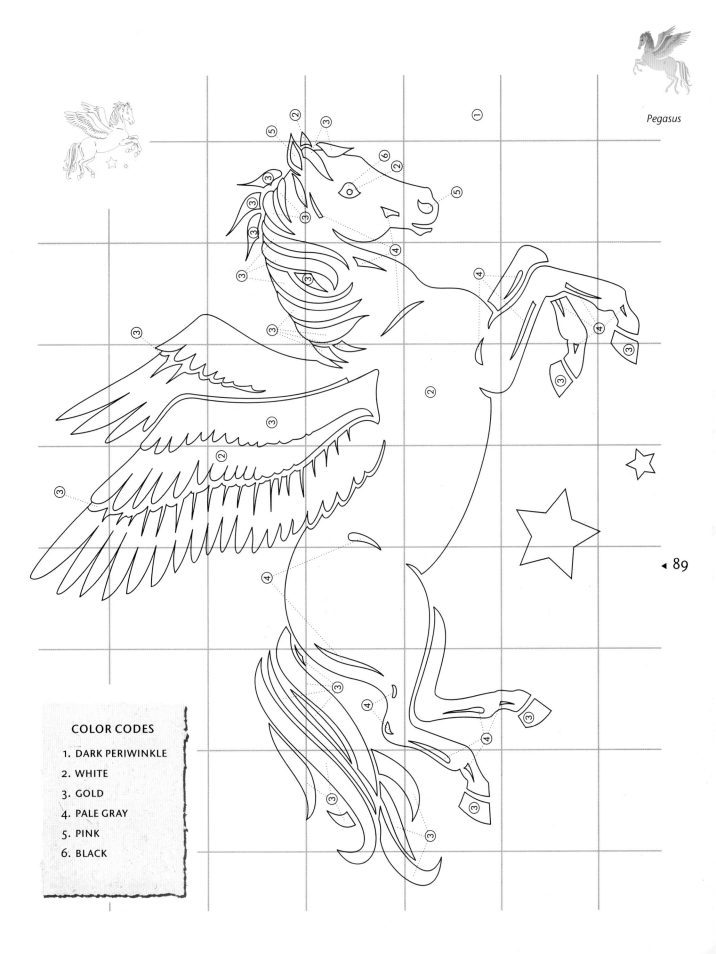

COLOR CODES

1. DARK PERIWINKLE
2. WHITE
3. GOLD
4. PALE GRAY
5. PINK
6. BLACK

◄ 89

Snowboarder

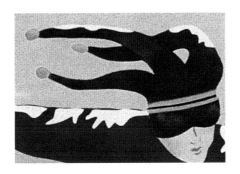

Young children are blissfully unsophisticated art critics. However, when creating for teenagers you have to realize that for a few brief years they know everything, so it is of utmost importance to involve them in the design and color selection of their mural. Leslie neglected to do this when she painted a surprise mural for her son, Danny, an avid snowboarder. He loved the design of the snowboarder, but his mother was obviously out of touch with "coolness" when it came to the boarder's clothing. The colors were all wrong! Leslie followed Danny's advice. Check out the dude's awesome new gear.

METHOD

1. Basecoat the wall with a white low-lustre latex paint. Let dry. Place your projected pattern on the wall. Cut along the line dividing the mountain range from the sky. Remove the entire upper section containing the sky and snowboarder. Save this piece.

2. Paint the background sky blue. Remember to use a dry roller technique as you near the edge of the freezer paper to prevent the paint from bleeding underneath. Don't agonize over this part as it will be background. Let the paint dry for at least four hours

3. Cut around the entire outline of the snowboarder and his board. Gently remove and save this large cutout. Leave the pieces marked

SPECIAL TOOLS & MATERIALS

- Five rollers (or one roller and four refills)
- Five stencil brushes of various sizes
- White, black, light gray, coral, purple, light blue, dark blue, flesh tone, yellow, and turquoise paint

See page 40 for details on
STANDARD TOOLS & MATERIALS

by an "X" on your line drawing in place. Run your fingers carefully around the cut edges to make sure they are stuck flat to the wall.

4. Using a stencil roller and white paint, roller stencil the snowboarder's body and board. You will require several coats of paint for good coverage. You may want to speed up this process with a hair dryer. When the paint is dry, replace the cutout section.

5. Cut out the light purple section of the mountain where the light purple color meets the snow line. Save this large cutout. (This piece will contain two of the dark purple cutouts.) Roller stencil this entire area light purple. Let it dry and replace this cutout.

6. Next cut out the dark purple mountain shadows. Stencil these areas dark purple.

7. Cut out the gloves, goggles, and boots and save these cutouts. Be careful to cut around and leave in the small white highlighted area on the glove. Stencil the gloves, boots and goggles black. Let the paint dry.

8. Reposition the cutouts of the gloves, goggles and boots of the snowboarder.

9. Cut out the jacket, being careful to cut around and leave the white highlighted areas stuck to the wall. Save the jacket cutout. Stencil the jacket coral. Shade under the arms and at the bottom of the jacket with a slightly darker coral (add a couple of drops of black to your coral paint). Let the paint dry and then reposition the jacket cutout.

10. Cut out the dark purple hat (not including the yellow pom-poms) being careful to cut around and leave in the white highlighted areas. Stencil it purple. Let it dry and replace the cutout. Cut along the dotted lines and flip these sections back so that you can shade along the freezer paper edge. (Add a few drops of black to your purple and use a small stencil brush) This is to enable the middle tail of the hat to appear in the foreground.

11. Cut out and stencil the pom-poms on the end of the hat. Using a stencil brush, color them yellow. Cut out the snowboarder's face and stencil it light flesh tone. Let paint dry and replace this cutout. Cut out his/her facial details and stencil these dark flesh tone.

13. Cut out the ski pants next. Start with the extended leg. Cut out this leg, being careful to cut around and leave the white highlighted areas affixed to the wall. Stencil the area turquoise. Using a stencil brush with very little paint shade the edge of the leg in the area where the two legs meet. Shade with a darker turquoise (add a few drops of black to your turquoise paint). Let the paint dry then reposition this leg piece.

14. Cut out the bent leg, being careful to leave the white highlighted areas in place. Save the cutout. Stencil this cutout turquoise. Let dry and reposition the bent leg cutout.

15. Cut along the dotted line (see color coded drawing) differentiating the leg from the seat of the pants. Keeping the rest of the stencil in place, carefully lift up the seat portion and stencil dark turquoise shading along the edge of the freezer paper.

16. Cut out the underside of the snowboard and the two yellow stripes above the goggles.

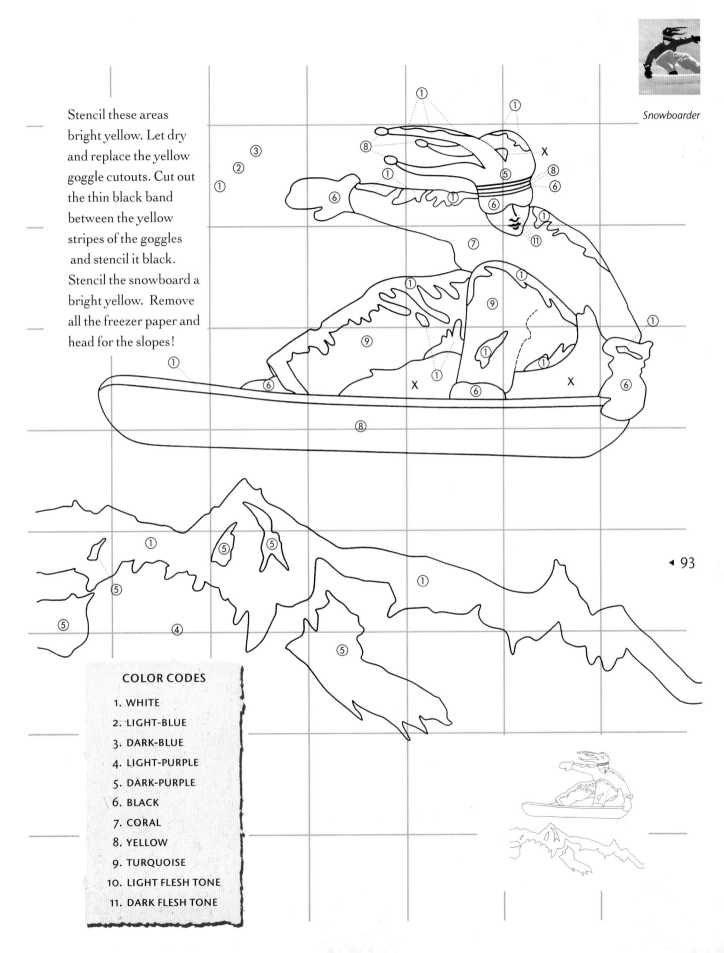

Stencil these areas bright yellow. Let dry and replace the yellow goggle cutouts. Cut out the thin black band between the yellow stripes of the goggles and stencil it black. Stencil the snowboard a bright yellow. Remove all the freezer paper and head for the slopes!

Snowboarder

◄ 93

COLOR CODES

1. WHITE
2. LIGHT-BLUE
3. DARK-BLUE
4. LIGHT-PURPLE
5. DARK-PURPLE
6. BLACK
7. CORAL
8. YELLOW
9. TURQUOISE
10. LIGHT FLESH TONE
11. DARK FLESH TONE

Monarch Butterfly & Fairy

*A*s a child, were you ever afraid to go to bed because of the monsters lurking under your bed, in your closet, or behind your curtain? With the Monarch Fairy looking over your little ones, they can kiss their bedtime fears good-bye.

METHOD

1. Cut out the mushroom caps, being careful to cut around the fairy's feet and the spots on the caps. Remove the cap cutouts, leaving behind the spots. Roller stencil the caps a golden terra-cotta using a paint mixture of half terra-cotta and half yellow, making sure to use a dry roller technique around the edges of the caps so the paint does not bleed under the freezer paper. Several coats of paint will be needed. Using a dry brush stencil technique, shade with terra-cotta around the outside edge of the caps. When the paint is dry, replace the mushroom cap cutouts. You may wish to speed up the drying process by using a hairdryer.

2. Cut out the mushroom stems and roller stencil them bone white. Shade with golden terra-cotta around the edges of these using a dry brush technique.

3. Cut out the entire butterfly. Remove this cutout and roller stencil the exposed area orange. Replace this cutout.

4. Cut out and remove all the black portions of the butterfly. Roller

SPECIAL TOOLS & MATERIALS

- Five stencil brushes of varying size
- Five stencil rollers (or one roller and four refills)
- Yellow, black, terra-cotta, dark flesh tone, bone white, orange, flesh tone, periwinkle, and dark periwinkle paint

See page 40 for details on
STANDARD TOOLS & MATERIALS

stencil these areas black. *Note:* Cut on both sides of the fine lines of the wings.

5. Cut out the fairy's dress and stencil this area periwinkle. Shade along the front of the dress, and the top and side of the sleeve with dark periwinkle using a dry brush technique. Replace the dress cutout once the paint dries.

6. Cut out all the flesh-colored sections and roller stencil these flesh tone. When the paint dries, reposition the upper arm only and shade around the edges of the lower arm with dark flesh tone. Replace the lower arm cutout and re-move the upper arm cutout. Shade around the outside of this cutout area and around the feet in a similar manner.

7. Replace the face section and carefully cut out the facial features. Stencil the eyebrow, mouth, and chin line a dark flesh tone. Mix a little black with the dark flesh tone for the eye color. Cut along the line under the fairy's chin and fold back the neck area so you can add a little dark flesh tone shading under her chin. Replace the face cutout once the paint dries.

8. Cut out the dark periwinkle sec-tions of the dress and roller stencil these a dark periwin-kle. Save the cutout that touches the wing and the hair and reposition this piece once the paint dries.

9. Cut out the fairy's hair and save this cutout. Using a brush, stencil her hair yellow. When the paint dries, reposition the hair and cut out the dark highlights. Stencil these a dark flesh color.

10. Cut out the sections of the wings, and using a dry brush technique, shade around the outside of these sections with dark periwinkle. If your wall is not white or off-white, you may wish to stencil the wing sections white before shading with periwinkle.

11. Remove all the freezer paper and admire!

Monarch
BUtterfly

COLOR CODES

1. GOLDEN TERRA COTTA
2. WHITE
3. ORANGE
4. BLACK
5. PERIWINKLE
6. FLESHTONE
7. DARK-FLESHTONE
8. VERY DARK-FLESHTONE
9. DARK-PERIWINKLE
10. BONE WHITE
11. YELLOW

◄ 97

DeHavilland "Tiger Moth" Airplane

Leslie and I are not airplane buffs, and the popularity of this mural caught us by surprise. We've had requests for it from seven-year-olds to eighty-year-olds.

It's a good thing our illustrator for this design, Edward Turner, knows more about airplanes than we do. When we originally wrote the instructions for this mural, one step read, "Cut out the side of the whatchamacallit in the center of the top wing, and roller stencil it with shadow glaze." Another step read, "Cut out all the black sections with the exception of the thingamajig on the forward post." Thanks to Ted, the "whatchamacallit" is now a fuel tank, and the "thingamajig" is now a pitot tube. We also discovered that the "horn" is an airspeed indicator! In case you are no more knowledgeable than we are about aircraft, we have labeled parts of the diagram to aid you in following our instructions.

METHOD

1. Cut out the wings and the main body of the airplane. In the process of cutting out these two sections, you will cut through the wing struts, and landing gear (see right). Roller stencil the exposed areas golden yellow.

◄ 99

See page 40 for details on
STANDARD TOOLS & MATERIALS

2. Using a 1" stencil brush and light yellow paint (golden yellow mixed with white) add some highlights along the top edge of the main body of the plane, between the passenger seat and the tail, using a very dry stenciling technique.

3. Once the paint has dried, replace the two large cutouts. You may wish to speed up the drying process by using a hairdryer.

4. Cut out the orange sections of the plane cutting right through the wing and wheel struts. Roller stencil these areas orange. Once the orange paint has dried, replace the cutouts.

5. Cut out the bottom panel of the plane's nose and the side of the fuel tank (located in the middle of the top wing) and stencil these with shadow glaze. Dry the glaze with a hairdryer, and replace the cutouts.

6. Cut out the faceplate on the nose of the plane, and the nose of the propeller. Leave the paper ring between the faceplate and the nose of the propeller in place. Roller stencil these areas gold. When the gold paint has dried, replace the cutouts.

7. Cut out all the black sections with the exception of the pitot tube on the forward strut and roller stencil these black. Replace the cutouts for the wheels, wheel struts, engine cover, and the pilot.

8. Cut out the golden yellow bars on the wheels and the wings. Before you stencil these sections yellow, use gesso or white paint to stencil over the orange showing through the cutout areas.

9. Stencil the bars golden yellow. With a ½" stencil brush, shade around the outside of these bars with dark golden yellow (add a little black to your golden yellow paint) to give them the illusion of roundness.

10. Reposition the forward wing strut closest to the propeller.

11. Cut out the shadows representing the propeller. Roller stencil these with shadow glaze.

12. Cut out the airspeed indicator. Use a small piece of painter's tape to prevent the indicator from joining up with the adjacent stripe. Stencil the indicator gold. When the gold paint dries, reposition the indicator, cut out the mouth of the indicator, and stencil it dark gold (created by adding a drop of black to your gold paint).

13. Cut out the pitot tube and stencil this area black.

14. Use your gray felt marker to apply definition lines on the body of the aircraft. Refer to the illustration for the location of these lines. Cut along these lines and then use a straight edge to guide your felt marker. We found it easier to use a straight edge as a guide rather than a cut paper edge when trying to draw a straight line with a marker.

15. Remove all the freezer paper.

16. With your gray felt marker and a straight edge, draw the guide wires on the craft.

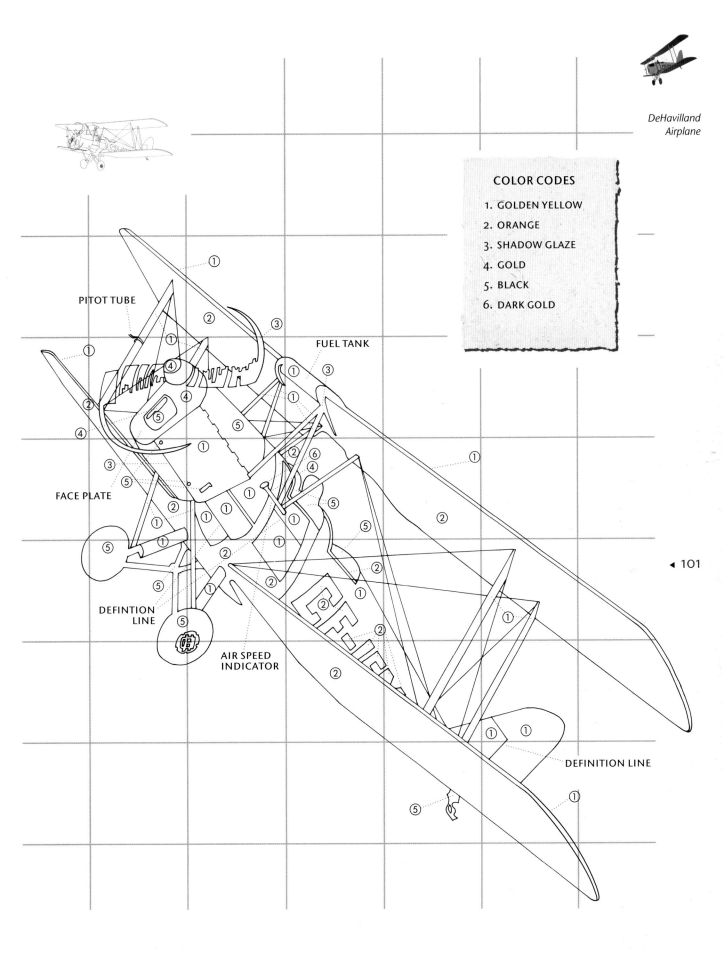

DeHavilland
Airplane

COLOR CODES

1. GOLDEN YELLOW
2. ORANGE
3. SHADOW GLAZE
4. GOLD
5. BLACK
6. DARK GOLD

PITOT TUBE

FUEL TANK

FACE PLATE

DEFINTION
LINE

AIR SPEED
INDICATOR

DEFINITION LINE

Tiger, Tiger

One would think my parents were longtime cat lovers with this giant tiger stenciled in a trompe l'oeil alcove painted above their bed, but the truth is, they dislike cats of any size. My husband, Greg, and I had our cat, Leroy, for twelve years before my mother even bothered to learn his name.

Things might have stayed that way had Greg and I not sold our home to move aboard a boat. You know the saying, "You can't teach an old dog new tricks"? Well, the same is apparently true of cats. We moved Leroy aboard *Inside Passage* and told him he was now the ship's cat, but he paid us no notice and made it clear he wasn't happy in his new surroundings. We asked my parents, who lived in a house, if they would take him and they flatly refused. As luck would have it, one day last September we were cruising off the coast of my parents' village, and Leroy lost his sea legs altogether. He looked so pitiful that we begged my parents to look after him for the two weeks we would be at sea. Now, six months later, we could not get Leroy back if we wanted. My parents have fallen in love with him even if they won't admit it.

When I asked my parents if I could paint a tiger over their bed for the book, my stepfather said sarcastically, "Why not? The bigger the better! We just love cats!" And do you know what? They love this guy too.

SPECIAL TOOLS & MATERIALS

- Five stencil rollers (or one roller and four refills)
- An assortment of stencil brushes (¾", ½", ¼")
- Paint the same color as the wall to be stenciled, as well as white, black, golden yellow, terracotta, golden orange, spring green, and forest green paint
- Blending glaze
- Shadow glaze (see page 23)
- Pencil

◄ 103

See page 40 for details on
STANDARD TOOLS & MATERIALS

METHOD

This mural is made up of three parts: the alcove, the tiger, and the greenery. You will need to stencil the alcove first, then remove the freezer paper to position the pattern for the tiger. Once the tiger has been stenciled, remove the paper and add the design for the greenery.

Alcove

1. Cover the wall with freezer paper using stencil spray adhesive, and project and trace the alcove image onto it. Fill in the back line of the alcove by joining line A and line B. Do not trace the tiger.

2. Cut along the line defining the outside of the alcove. Remove the cutout piece and roller stencil the exposed area several shades lighter than the wall color. (We mixed one part wall color paint with one part white paint.) Replace the cutout once the paint has dried. You can speed up the drying process using a hairdryer.

3. Cut out the section representing the floor of the alcove. Stencil this area still lighter. (We used one part wall color to three parts white paint.) When the paint is dry, replace the cutout.

4. Cut along the line defining the subtle shadow on the back of the alcove and remove the cutout piece. Roller stencil the opening lightly with shadow glaze and replace this cutout once glaze has dried.

5. Remove the freezer paper surrounding the alcove and shade around the outside of the alcove with paint that is slightly darker than your wall color. I simply added a bit of black paint to the wall paint.

6. Further define the lines of the alcove by tracing them with a pencil.

Tiger

1. Project and trace the tiger pattern onto freezer paper positioned in the alcove. Cut around the outline of the tiger's body. Remove the cutout and save it to use later. Stencil the tiger's body light golden yellow. Then, using a large stencil brush, shade around the outside of the tiger's body using terra-cotta paint. Once the paint has dried (you may wish to use a hairdryer to speed drying), replace the cutout of the tiger's body.

2. Cut out the three white sections around the tiger's face (side tuftsas and chin) and stencil these areas white. Fold back the inside cut edge of the side tuft and use a dry brush pouncing technique to add more white to the tiger's face. Fade out your pouncing as you move toward the center of his face because you want a soft outline for these white sections, not a hard edge. Replace the cutouts.

3. Cut out along dotted lines and softly pounce in white highlights. Keep the edges soft for these sections by not pouncing right to the edge of the cutout. Replace the cutouts.

4. Cut out the green of the tiger's eyes. Stencil the eyes spring green. Replace the cutouts once the paint dries.

5. Cut out the black sections of the tiger and roller stencil them orange-black (we used one part black to one part golden orange). These sections will look quite black even though you have mixed the black with orange.

6. Using a very dry brush stenciling technique, add light golden yellow highlights to the black sections. See the photo for suggested placement of the highlights.

7. Remove the freezer paper and shade the golden sections of the tiger with golden orange and terra-cotta paint mixed with glaze. It is important that you mix glaze with your paint so that your shading appears translucent. Refer to the photo for placement of the shading.

Greenery

1. Cut out the greenery and roller stencil it spring green.

2. Using a ½" stencil brush, shade the leaves with forest green.

3. Using a ¼" stencil brush shade around the outside edges of the stems with forest green and terra-cotta.

4. Remove the freezer paper.

5. Sleep well knowing you are well protected!

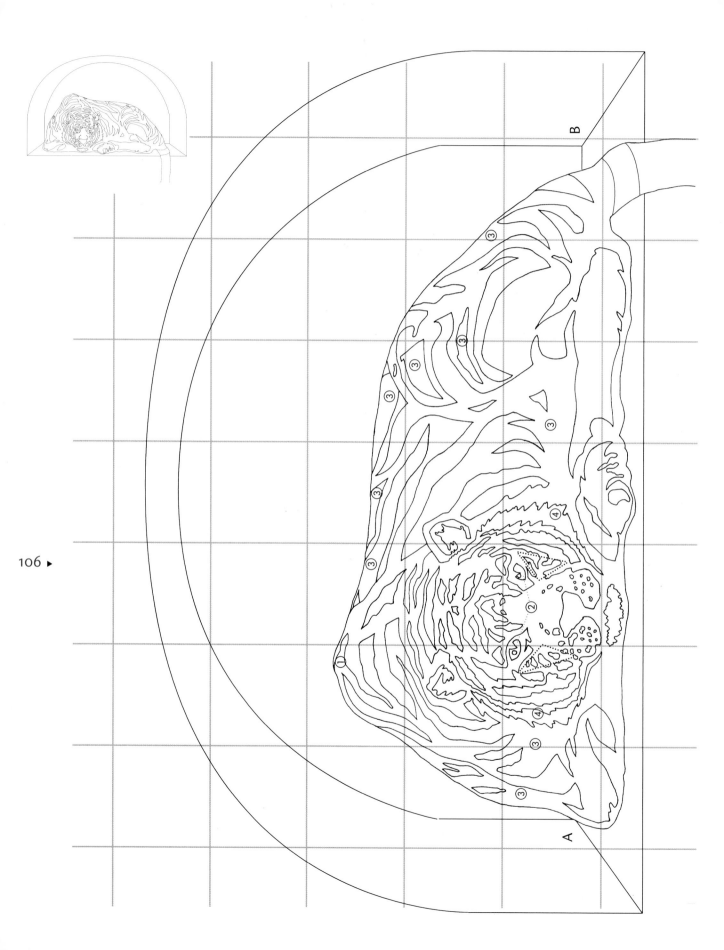

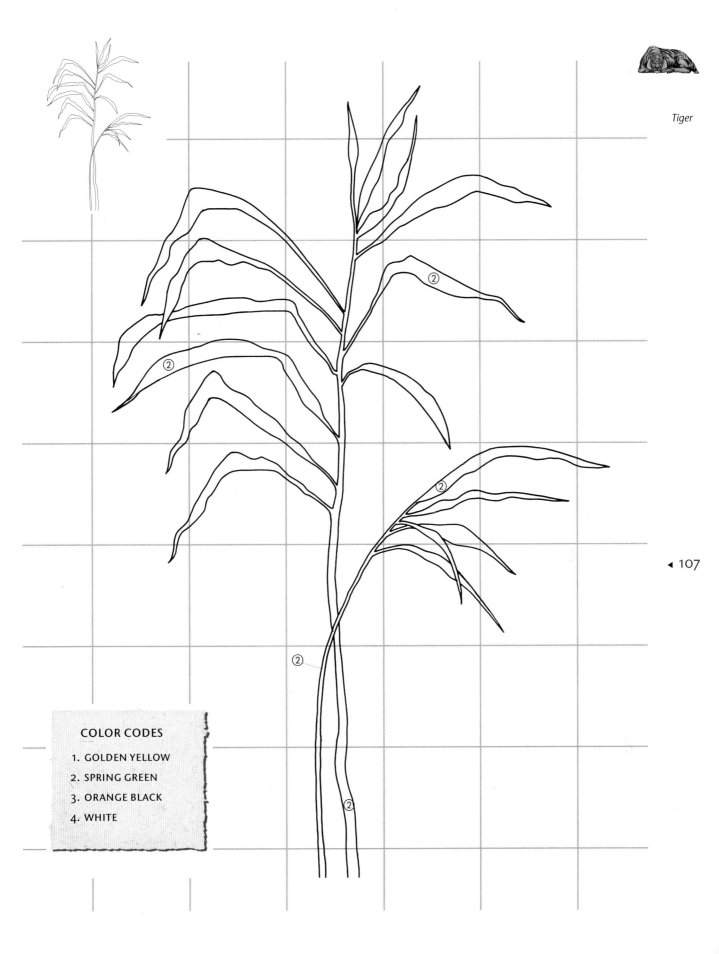

COLOR CODES

1. GOLDEN YELLOW
2. SPRING GREEN
3. ORANGE BLACK
4. WHITE

Alice in Wonderland & the White Rabbit

SPECIAL TOOLS & MATERIALS

- Five stencil rollers (or one roller and four refills)
- Stencil brushes (three ½" brushes, three ¼" brushes, one ⅝" brush, and one 1" brush)
- Blending glaze
- Ruler
- Pencil
- Painter's tape
- Periwinkle, gold, purple, gray white, black, pink, flesh tone, brown, terracotta, yellow, golden orange, and blue paint (*for Alice*)
- Black, white, light gray, gray, light red, dark red, gold, light tan, dark tan, pink, light purple, and dark purple paint (*for the Rabbit*)

See page 40 for details on STANDARD TOOLS & MATERIALS

In the studio, Leslie and I worked side by side on the Alice in Wonderland designs. While Leslie worked on the White Rabbit, I stenciled Alice. Apparently our memory of the much-loved children's book by Lewis Carroll was a little rusty. This became evident as we got down to the final color choices. We decided, after some debate, to paint in purple what we thought was a yo-yo hanging from the rabbit's paw. Later, we changed our minds and repainted it blue to match Alice's dress. We were so intent on admiring the results of our work that we were late for an appointment with our editor, Susan. It wasn't until then that we remembered the beginning of the tale of *Alice in Wonderland*. She wakes up from a nap and sees the White Rabbit standing at the entrance of a rabbit hole, holding a pocket watch (and not a yo-yo!) and saying "I'm late! I'm late! For a very important date!" Not wanting to put a new "spin" on the story of Alice in Wonderland, we changed the watch to gold.

METHOD *for Alice*

1. Cut out the periwinkle sections of Alice's dress and roller stencil these periwinkle. When the paint dries, replace the cutouts. You may

wish to use a hairdryer to speed the drying process.

2. Cut along the two folds in the periwinkle section of Alice's skirt and shade along these folds using a stencil brush and dark periwinkle paint (created by adding a drop of black to the periwinkle). Similarly, cut along the sleeve seams, and shade along the inside of the seams with dark peri-winkle.

3. Remove the periwinkle sections of the dress and shade around the outside edge of the dress with dark periwinkle. Replace the dress cutouts.

4. Cut out the gold sections of the dress and stencil them gold. When the paint has dried, replace the cutouts.

5. Cut out the purple fringes of the skirt, and roller stencil them purple. Replace this cutout once the paint has dried.

6. Cut out and remove the white sleeve puffs. Shade gray around the outer edges of the sleeves. Replace these cutouts once the paint has dried.

7. Cut around the outside of the pink sections of the flamingo, being careful to cut out around the flamingo's eye. Leave the pattern for the eye in place when you remove the freezer paper. Roller stencil the flamingo pink and shade around the outside dark pink (created by adding a drop or two of black to the pink). Replace these cutouts once the paint has dried.

8. Cut out the wing detail and stencil the detail dark pink with a ½" stencil brush.

9. Cut out and remove the sections of the design marked flesh tone, being careful to cut around the outside of Alice's eyeball and to leave this piece of the pattern in place as a mask. Roller stencil the flesh tone sections and shade with brown around the outside edges of these sections using ½" and ¼" brushes.

10. Replace the face cutout and cut along the chin line. Shade brown under the chin.

11. Replace the leg cutout and cut along the line separating the legs. Remove the back leg cutout and using a ½" stencil brush, shade with brown along the left side of the back leg. Reposition the back leg cutout once the paint dries.

12. Replace the forward arm cutout and cut along the arm fold. Using your ½" stencil brush, shade with brown along the top of the forearm.

13. Cut out the flamingo's legs, including the joints and the claws, and the flamingo's beak. Stencil these golden orange (half yel-

Note: These instructions assume that the wall is basecoated with low-luster latex white paint.

low, half terra-cotta) using a roller or a 1" stencil brush. Using a ¼" stencil brush, shade the outside edge of the legs terra-cotta. Using a ½" brush, shade around the outside edge of the feet and the beak. Replace the leg cutouts once the paint has dried. Cut out the claws and stencil them brown.

14. Cut out the flamingo's leg joints and stencil the exposed area terra-cotta. Shade around the outside edges of the joints with dark terra-cotta (created by adding a little black to the terra-cotta). Replace the joint cutout and cut along the line separating the foreground joint from the background joint. Leave the front joint in place, and shade with dark terra-cotta along this cutline.

15. Cut out Alice's hair, and roller stencil the exposed area yellow. Replace the hair cutout. Cut out the hair highlights, and using a ½" stencil brush, stencil these brown.

16. Cut out the iris of Alice's eye. Stencil it blue. Once the paint has dried, replace the iris. cut out the pupil and stencil it black. Add a white highlight to the pupil with a dab of white paint. Replace the pupil cutout.

17. Cut out Alice's facial definition. This includes her lips, eyebrows, nose shadow, eyelids and lashes. Use a small stencil brush to stencil these areas brown.

18. Add a bit of color to Alice's cheeks by rubbing on a little pink paint with a stencil brush.

19. Cut out Alice's shoes and stencil them black. Once the paint has dried, reposition the shoe cutouts.

20. Cut out around the outside edge of the porcupines and roller stencil the exposed area brown. Shade dark brown (half black, half brown) around the outside edge of the porcupines, making sure to prominently shade the porcupine's nose.

21. Replace the cutout of the large porcupine and cut along the line that defines the porcupines' back. Remove and save the top cutout, leaving the belly and front leg in place. Shade dark brown along the top of the belly. You can create a mottled appearance on the porcupine's back and the rolled up porcupine by stenciling in the areas with a 1" brush and using a pouncing technique to apply dark brown paint.

22. Cut between the porcupine's front toes and flip the toes up one at a time to shade dark brown between the toes.

23. Replace the top cutout of the porcupine. Cut out the eye, and stencil this area black.

24. Cut along the line that separates the head from the rest of the body. Shade along the "neck" line with dark brown paint.

25. Use a ruler and a pencil to draw two little lines on Alice's skirt where white meets white.

METHOD *for Rabbit*

1. Basecoat your wall to be stenciled with a white low-luster latex. Let it dry overnight.
2. Position your White Rabbit design on the wall.

3. Cut out the rabbit's head, including the foreground ear, but not the background ear. *Note:* You will be cutting through the trumpet and whiskers as you follow the contours of his face. Save this cutout.

4. Use a ½" stencil brush and light gray paint to shade around the outer edge of the rabbit's face.

5. Replace the cutout to its exact original position. Cut, remove, and save the pink piece of the ear. Roller stencil this area pink. Let dry and replace this piece.

6. Next, cut out all the light gray areas, including the distant ear, chin and cheek lines, two rear sections of the banner hanging on the trumpet, and the underside of the sleeve with the ribbon on it. Replace all of these gray cutouts except for the distant ear, the chin line, and the cheek line. Cut out the hand holding the trumpet, finger by finger. Shade around the outside of each finger, and replace each finger segment as you go. Cut out the thumb and inside of the paw and shade with light gray around those areas. Cut out the hand holding the scroll and shade light gray around the outside of it. Cut out and stencil the belly of the rabbit light gray. Let these areas dry, and then replace all the pieces.

7. Cut out and save the rabbit's two legs and roller stencil them gray. Let the paint dry and replace these pieces.

8. Cut out the red heart pieces next. Save the two heart pieces that are not surrounded entirely by white, and discard the other eight. Roller stencil these areas red. Cut out and stencil the red areas of the rabbit's cape and save the pieces. Replace the pieces when the paint is dry. Cut out and save the red sleeve piece beside the trumpet banner. Roller stencil this area red, let the paint dry, and replace the piece. Next, cut around the entire outside edge of the bow and save the cutout. Stencil the area light red, shading with darker red near the end of the ribbon with a ½" stencil brush. Create a dark red by adding a drop of black paint. Let the paint dry and replace the cutout (cut out the circular knot in the bow and stencil it dark red). Cut out the inside of the bow, and discard this piece. Stencil this area dark red.

9. Cut out the gold sections next. Start with the gold band around the outside of the cape and the fringe. Save only the pieces that are touching the purple collar, sleeve, and scroll. Using a 5/8" stencil brush stencil these gold. Replace the saved cutouts when the paint is dry. Cut out the trumpet in one piece by cutting through the black "strings" circling it. Using a ½" stencil brush, stencil this area gold. Let the paint dry and replace the cutout. Cut out the trumpet opening and stencil it dark gold (created by adding a few drops of black to your gold paint). Let the paint dry and replace this piece. Cut out the watch and strap, saving the cutout. Stencil the area gold, let the paint dry, and replace the cutout. Cut out and discard the thin outer edge of the watch and stencil the area dark gold. Cut out the banner tassels and stencil them gold.

10. Cut out the neck ruffle by cutting around the entire ruffle. Save the cutout. Stencil the area light purple using a stencil brush. Let

dry and replace. Cut out the small figure eight shapes and discard them. Using a ½" stencil brush, stencil these areas dark purple. Cut out the sleeve and its ruffle as one piece. Remove and save the cutout. Using a stencil roller, paint the area light purple. Let the paint dry and replace the cutout. Cut out the sleeve and small ovals, and stencil them dark purple.

11. Cut out around the entire scroll, including cutting through the watch strap, and save this piece. Using a stencil roller, paint the area light tan. Let the paint dry and replace the cutout. Cut out and discard the underflap and coiled area of the scroll and, using a ½" stencil brush, paint the area dark tan.

12. Finally, cut out and stencil the black sections, including the eye, whiskers, nose, and banner strings. Remove all of the freezer paper.

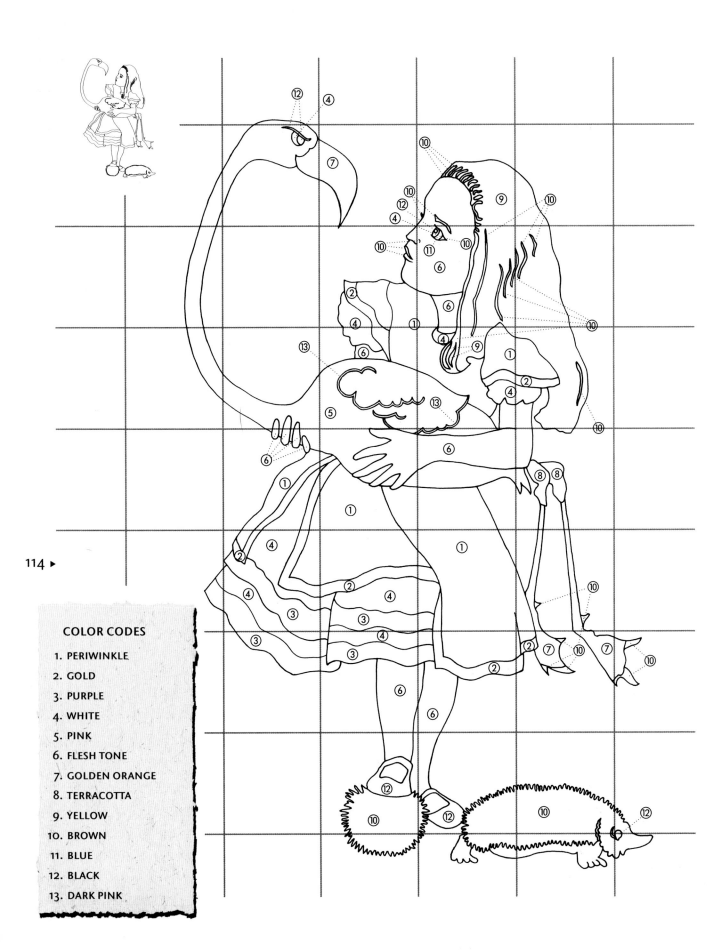

COLOR CODES

1. PERIWINKLE
2. GOLD
3. PURPLE
4. WHITE
5. PINK
6. FLESH TONE
7. GOLDEN ORANGE
8. TERRACOTTA
9. YELLOW
10. BROWN
11. BLUE
12. BLACK
13. DARK PINK

114 ▶

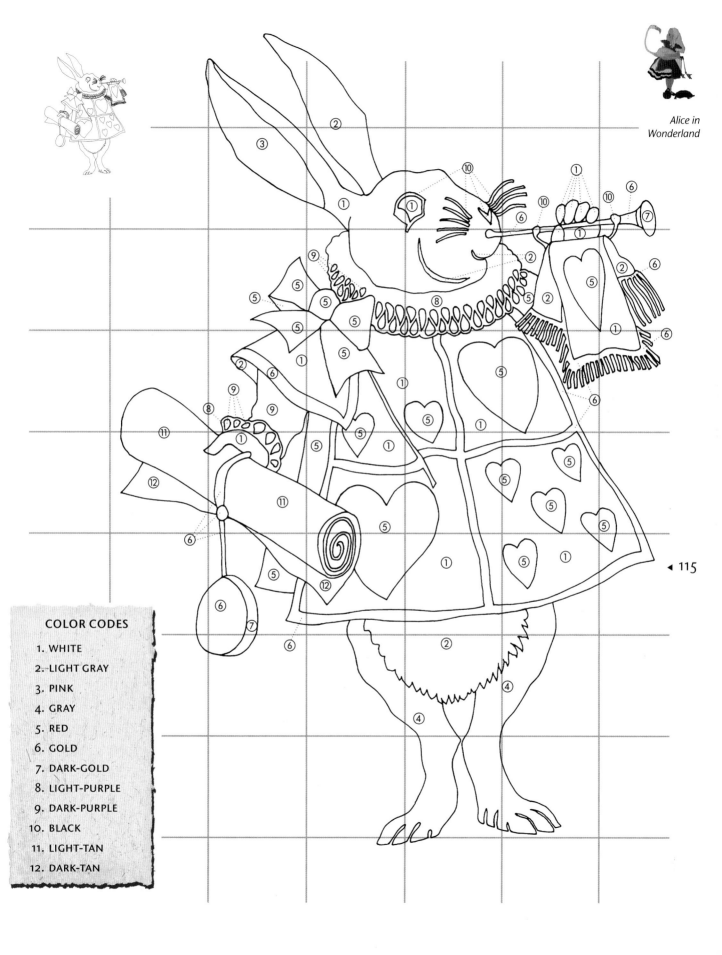

Alice in
Wonderland

◄ 115

COLOR CODES

1. WHITE
2. LIGHT GRAY
3. PINK
4. GRAY
5. RED
6. GOLD
7. DARK-GOLD
8. LIGHT-PURPLE
9. DARK-PURPLE
10. BLACK
11. LIGHT-TAN
12. DARK-TAN

Dragon

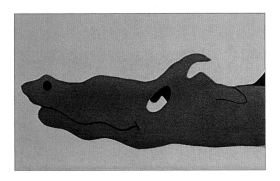

Leslie and I had a difficult time deciding on a fantasy figure suitable for a mural in a child's room. We dismissed one suggestion after another. The story of the Frog and the Princess wouldn't work because of the common problem of telling the difference between a frog and a prince. Cinderella stereotypes the step-family, and Godzilla would make it difficult for the kids to relax enough to close their eyes. We finally settled on a friendly dragon. Who could object to this gentle soul? We portrayed him with his head lowered so your child could whisper into his ear and share his hopes and dreams.

METHOD

1. To create a golden glow behind your castle, cut out the skyline by cutting around the landforms, the castle, and the dragon. Remove the sky cutout. Using a large stencil brush and a dry stenciling technique, stencil the yellow glow behind the castle. You may wish to speed up the drying process by using a hair dryer. Replace the sky cutout.

2. Cut out the landforms, cutting around the outside of the dragon's body in the process. Remove the landform cutouts, leaving the dragon in place. Roller stencil the landforms spring green. Once the spring green paint is dry, replace the landform cutouts.

3. Cut out the section containing the castle. Roller stencil this area light

◄ 117

SPECIAL TOOLS & MATERIALS

- Four stencil rollers, or one roller and and three refills
- Six brushes in a variety of sizes (¾", ⅝", and ½")
- Primary green, dark yellow, dark green, red, pale yellow, white, black, yellow, spring green, light purple, and blue paint

See page 40 for details on
STANDARD TOOLS & MATERIALS

purple. Once the light purple paint is dry replace the castle cutout.

4. Cut out around the dragon's spikes on his back and in the process, cut along the line that separates his spikes from his back. Do not remove the spike cutouts.

5. Cut out around the outside of all the remaining primary green sections of the dragon. Remove this large cutout being careful to leave the dragon's spikes and belly affixed to the wall.

6. Roller stencil the dragon primary green.

7. Using a dry brush stenciling technique and white paint, add highlights to the top of the dragon's body. See the photograph for where to place the highlights. Again, using a dry brush stenciling technique, add dark green shading under the dragon's chin, feet, and tail. Once the green paint is dry, replace the cutout of the dragon's body.

8. Cut out the dragon's wing that appears nearest to you and the dragon's legs. With dark green paint and using a dry brush technique, shade along the base of the dragon's wing and around the outer edge of the dragon's legs. Refer to the photo for where to place the shading. Replace the leg cutouts and the wing cutout.

9. Cut along the little line that separates the front feet, and flipping up the background foot, shade dark green along this line.

10. Cut out the dark green sections of the wing and the spikes on the dragon's back. Stencil these areas dark green.

11. Cut out the dragon's spots and stencil these yellow. Cut out the dragon's toenails and the white of his eye and stencil these white using a stencil brush. Replace the eye cutout.

12. Cut out the dark lines defining the dragon's mouth and ear. Cut out the nostril and eyelid. Stencil these areas dark green. Replace his eyelid and cut out the dragon's iris. Stencil the iris black.

13. Remove the two sections of the dragon's yellow underbelly. Roller stencil these areas yellow.

14. Shade, using a stencil brush, along the bottom edge of the belly using dark yellow paint.

15. Once the yellow paint dries, replace the cutouts and cut out the dark lines defining the segments of the dragon's belly. Stencil these areas dark yellow.

16. Cut out around the outside of the bird's body. Using a brush or roller, stencil the bird blue, adding other colors if you wish. Once the blue paint dries, replace the bird cutout.

17. Cut out the bird's eye, beak, and the defining lines of the bird's feathers and wings. Stencil these areas black.

18. Cut out the flowers and stencil these the color of your choice. Depending on the color you choose, you may need to stencil the flowers white before topcoating them with your color.

19. Replace the flower cutouts and cut out the centers of the flowers. Stencil the centers a darker color than the petals.

20. Remove the freezer paper.

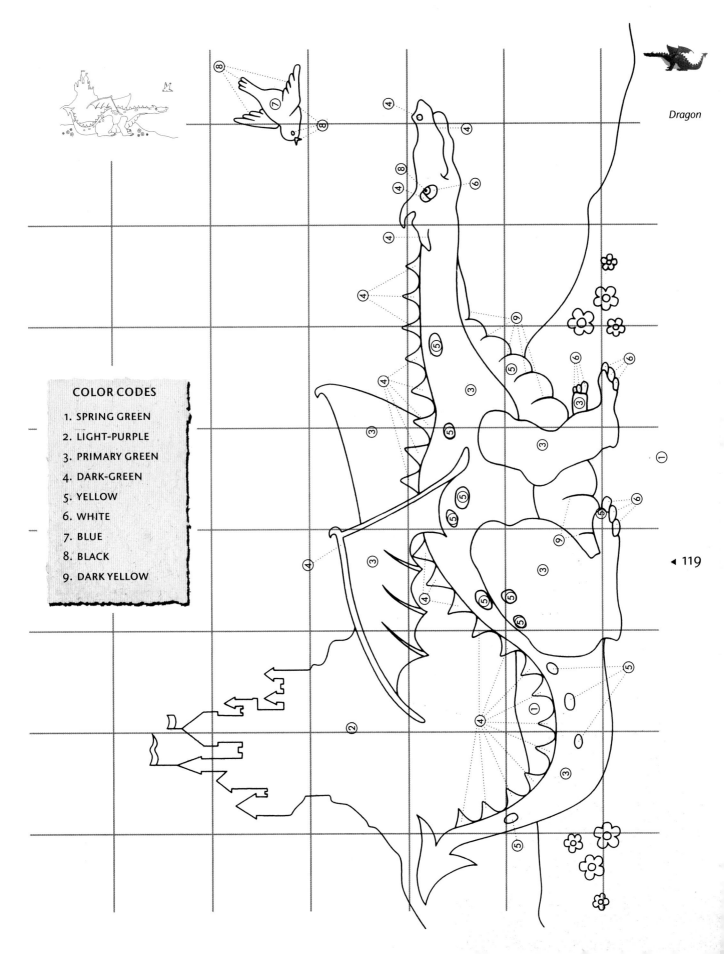

Dragon

COLOR CODES

1. SPRING GREEN
2. LIGHT-PURPLE
3. PRIMARY GREEN
4. DARK-GREEN
5. YELLOW
6. WHITE
7. BLUE
8. BLACK
9. DARK YELLOW

◄ 119

Tunnel Vision

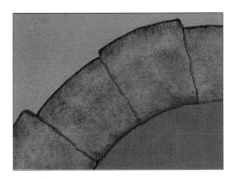

We painted this train and trestle for Claudia, the two-year-old daughter of a dear friend. We wanted to have the train run the length of the wall, but puzzled over how to incorporate the train into the rest of the room. I thought that putting a mirror at the end of the track on the adjacent wall was a brilliant idea. The continuity of the railway track wouldn't be broken, even though the wall had ended. It would proceed into infinity! Leslie and I stenciled the train and the bridge and then, the crowning touch, held up the mirror to position it on the wall. We immediately burst out laughing. What we saw was two trains about to have a head-on collision! We rethought the mirror and replaced it with a stenciled tunnel.

METHOD

1. Basecoat the walls to be stenciled with a low-luster latex paint.

2. Cut out the gray sections of the trestle bridge and roller stencil these gray. It will take several coats of gray to build up to the desired intensity. Replace the cutout for the portion of the track that goes through the tunnel.

3. Use painter's tape to mask off the top of the track where it comes in contact with the train.

4. Cut out the red section of the caboose, cutting along the outside line of the window. Remove the red section, leaving the paper pattern for the window affixed to the wall. Cut out the red of the coal car,

SPECIAL TOOLS & MATERIALS

- Five stenciling rollers (or one roller and four re-fills)
- An assortment of stenciling brushes
- White, black, gray, primary red, green, and blue, gold, yellow, taupe and golden yellow paint
- Shadow glaze (see page 23)
- Small aerosol can of gray spray paint
- Gray felt marker

See page 40 for details on
STANDARD TOOLS & MATERIALS

similarly cutting around the yellow border and leaving the yellow border and green panel attached to the wall. Save these cutouts. Cut out the red bow on the gift and the red balloon. Discard these cutouts. Stencil all these exposed areas red. Once the paint has dried, replace the caboose and the coal car pieces.

5. Cut out the green sections of the train (the window frame of the caboose, the seat of the passenger car, the green panel of the coal car, the gift, and the balloon). Throw away the window frame cutout and the balloon cutout, but save the other three cutout pieces. Stencil the exposed areas green, and when the paint dries, replace the passenger car seats, coal car panel, and present cutouts.

6. Cut out the blue of the caboose, freight car, balloon, and passenger car. Save the freight car cutout. Stencil these areas blue. Once the blue paint is dry, replace the freight car cutout.

7. Cut out the teddy and stencil it golden yellow and shade it with terra-cotta. Once the paint is dry, replace the teddy cutout. Cut out the teddy's bow tie and stencil it red. Cut out the teddy's facial features and stencil them black. Cut out the gold bands on the freight car and stencil them gold

8. Cut out the hobby horse and stencil it white. Replace the cutout. Cut out and stencil the horse's mane black. Replace the mane cutout piece and cut out the bridle. Stencil the bridle golden yellow.

9. Cut out the black sections of the train, including the engine (leave wall colored detail affixed to the wall), wheels, and the

coal. Save the engine cutout. Stencil the exposed areas black, and once the paint is dry, replace the engine cutout.

10. Cut out the gold and red details on the engine, cutting along the outside line of the red panel border. Save the panel cutout. Stencil these sections gold. Once the gold paint has dried, replace the panel cutout piece and cut out the red border. Stencil the exposed area red.

11. If you wish to paint a name on the coal car, trace and cut a small stencil (see page 73 for instructions).

12. Cut out the inside of the tunnel and save the cutout. Roller stencil the opening with shadow glaze. Once the glaze is dry, replace the cutout. Glaze dries slowly, so you may wish to speed up the process with a hairdryer.

13. Cut out the stone arch opening and discard the cutout. Roller stencil the stone white and dab on taupe, black, and white, using a sea sponge. While the paint is still wet, run a dry roller over the stone to roughly blend the colors. With a gray permanent felt marker, trace around the outside and inside edges of the stone arch. Use the same marker to draw.in freehand the mortar lines between the stones. Don't worry if your lines are a bit wobbly. This will only make your mortar lines more realistic.

14. Using a gray felt marker, freehand strings to the balloons.

15. Spray on small puffs of smoke using a can of spray paint. Don't enjoy this too much. I think this may be how graffiti artists start out!

CLAUDIA

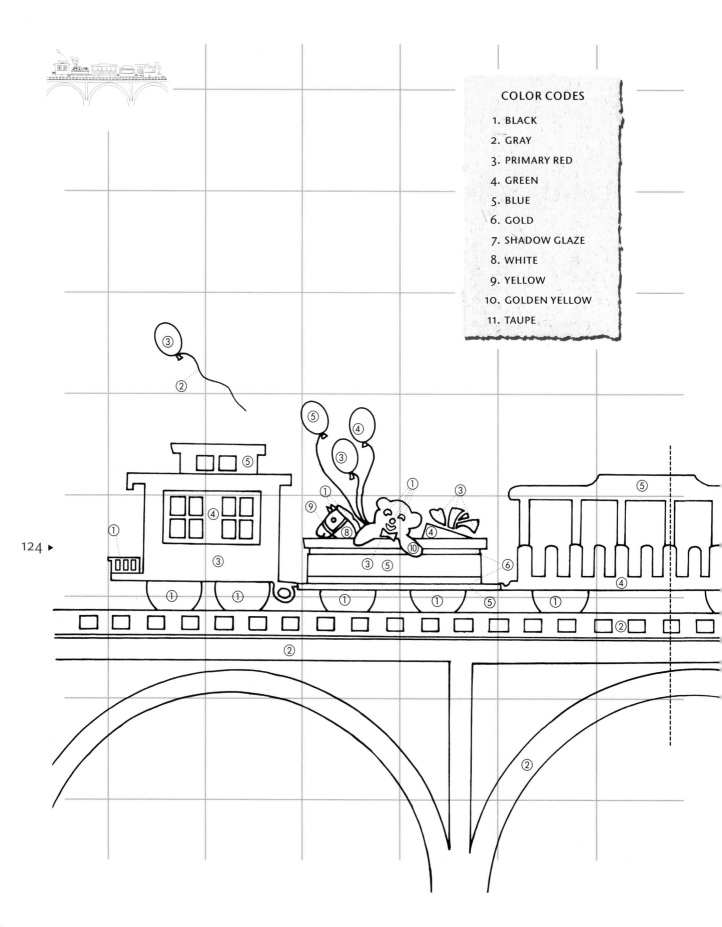

COLOR CODES

1. BLACK
2. GRAY
3. PRIMARY RED
4. GREEN
5. BLUE
6. GOLD
7. SHADOW GLAZE
8. WHITE
9. YELLOW
10. GOLDEN YELLOW
11. TAUPE

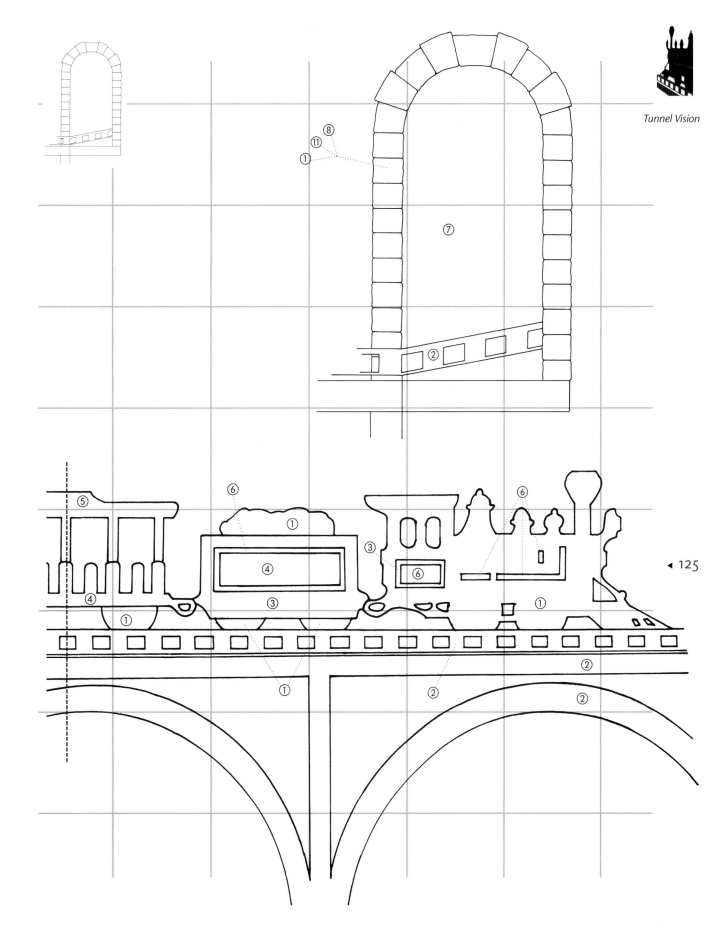

Tunnel Vision

◄ 125

Merlin Teddy

What child doesn't like magic? And what a magician Merlin is! He can perform countless acts of magic and even make himself disappear. Now you see him, now you don't!

We used a fabric blind for this project and it stenciled beautifully. Stenciling on a fabric surface is a little different than stenciling on a wall. Because the fabric is more absorbent than a wall surface, you will use more paint in your stencilling. Be careful when cutting out your design, because it is very easy to cut through the fabric. We recommend lifting the freezer paper slightly with a finger when cutting out your design so you are not cutting directly on the blind.

METHOD

1. Measure your blind and cut a piece of freezer paper the same dimensions as the blind.

2. Using stencil adhesive, stick the freezer paper on a wall, project the image on the paper, and trace your pattern.

3. Lay the blind on a table and cover it with the freezer paper pattern.

4. Begin by cutting out all the blue pieces. Cut around the outside of the hat and around the moon and the star. Remove the hat (saving the cutout), but leave the star and the moon attached to the blind. Cut out the blue sections of the robe and cut around the star belt buckle. Re-

---

SPECIAL TOOLS & MATERIALS

- A white blind that fits the window you want to cover (fabric is best)
- Two stencil foam rollers
- One ½" stencil brush, and two 1" stencil brushes
- Blue, terra-cotta, black, white, and gold paint

See page 40 for details on
STANDARD TOOLS & MATERIALS

move the robe pieces (including the black belt), but leave the star buckle attached to the blind. Roller stencil these areas blue. If you wish, you can add shading using dark blue, or highlighting using light blue, to the robe using a 1″ stencil brush and a very dry brush technique.

5. Replace the robe piece which contains the belt and replace the hat cutout.

6. Remove the star buckle, saving the cutout, and the moon and the stars on the hat. Cut out and remove the six stars Merlin is juggling. Roller stencil these areas gold.

7. Once the gold paint is dry, replace the star buckle cutout. Cut out the black sections the belt and Merlin's eyes and nose. Stencil these areas black. Place small white dots in Merlin's eyes as shown in the photograph.

The wooden end of a small artist's brush works well for this.

8. Cut out all the terra cotta areas and stencil these using a 1″ stencil brush. You may wish to shade around the outside of these cutouts using a ½″ brush and dark terra cotta paint. Remove all the freezer paper.

9. As a finishing touch, you may want to paint a 1″ band of gold around the outside edge of the blind.

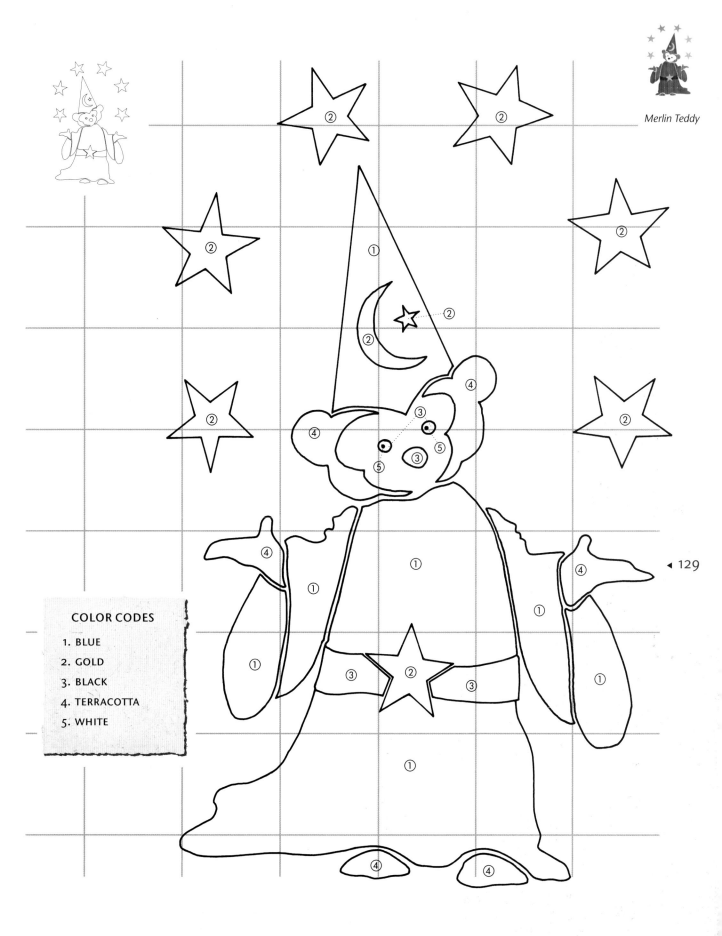

Merlin Teddy

◀ 129

COLOR CODES

1. BLUE
2. GOLD
3. BLACK
4. TERRACOTTA
5. WHITE

Chalkboard Silhouette
The Writing on the Wall

 ome of my fondest memories as a child were playing in my grandparents' backyard. In the summertime my sister, Sandra, and I delighted in running through the garden sprinkler. Now and then the clip-clop of the horse coming down the lane to make milk deliveries interrupted our play, and we would rush to our grandmother to get apples to feed him. But even more special than the sprinkler and the horse was something else in my grandparents' backyard—a garage. There Sandra and I got to do what children are never supposed to. We got to draw on the walls. Sometimes we used pencil, sometimes chalk, and on very special occasions, colored chalk.

It is ironic that, these many decades later, my sister and I find ourselves in the stencil business. I guess that the writing was on the wall! I know that the room pictured here would have been heaven when I was a child. The entire silhouette of the village is painted with chalkboard paint and invites children to express themselves in art.

METHOD

1. To create the background sky, basecoat the wall light sky blue. If you wish to add clouds, see instructions for painting the sky in Project 9, *Cow Jumping Over the Moon*.

SPECIAL TOOLS & MATERIALS

- One stencil roller
- One ½" stencil brush
- One regular paint roller
- One paint brush (for cutting in)
- Chalkboard paint (we used royal blue)
- Royal blue latex paint (matte finish)

See page 40 for details on
STANDARD TOOLS & MATERIALS

132 ▸

2. Affix freezer paper to the lower half of the walls to be stenciled and project the image onto the paper. Trace the outline of the village. If you are stenciling the skyline on more than one wall, simply move the projector so that the outlines are aligned and the image runs smoothly from one wall to the next. Each section of the skyline is designed to meet up with the others in the middle. With a sharp X-acto® or utility knife, cut along the skyline of the village. Remove the freezer paper below the skyline.

3. Paint the area below the skyline royal blue. We used royal blue latex low-luster paint to basecoat this area (it is much cheaper than chalkboard paint), and then topcoated it with two coats of chalkboard paint. Roller stencil along the cut edge of the freezer paper, then paint the remainder of the area with a regular paint brush and roller.

4. Follow the directions on the chalkboard paint can for drying time and for instructions on how to prepare the surface to be drawn on.

5. Add the wind vane and the cat to the design by making your own small stencil. Photocopy the full sized line drawings provided and cut your own stencil. Position the accent stencils on the rooftops and stencil them in using a ½" brush and chalkboard paint.

6. Let your little ones draw to their hearts' content.

①

◄ 133

①

COLOR CODES

1. ROYAL BLUE.

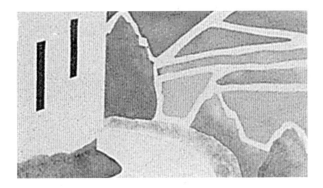

PART IV

Magnificent Murals

*H*ave you ever looked at photographs of beau tiful wall murals in glossy decorating maga zines and thought, "I wish I could do that!"? If your drawing ability falls in the "stick-man" category, you don't have a background in decorative painting, or any formal art training, then you would consider it ridiculous to even try painting an elaborate mural.

Well, the good news for you is that neither of us has had any special training and we are certainly not naturally "gifted" artistically (just ask our Grade Eight art teacher, Mrs. Boone). So if we can produce the murals in this book and make them look as if they have been painted by a professional artist (without the outrageous fee), then so can you.

Arbor

When my niece, Melanie, asked if she could get married in our house, I thought, "What fun!" A few days before the wedding Melanie asked me what I thought would be a good setting for the wedding photos. The wedding was set for early March, and although we on the West Coast smugly refer to our corner of the country as Lotus Land, the truth is that our weather can be quite unpleasant at that time of year. So, caught up in the spirit of the moment, I cheerfully volunteered to paint a garden room mural as a backdrop for the photos.

May I suggest that you don't do what I did. I found that undertaking a large-scale project I hadn't previously tried, and setting a crucial deadline, wasn't a great idea. I allowed myself about ten days to complete the mural and prepare for the wedding, which, when considering my busy work schedule and my domestic duties, wasn't much time. As the deadline approached, I was caught uttering profanities I hadn't used since my days running a fishing boat on the East Coast. Alice, a foreign student boarding with us at the time, asked in a confused voice, "Don't you and your sister write books about how easy and how much fun stenciling is?" She had me there.

I made the project more difficult than it needed to be. To project the arbor, I used the small Artograph®, which could only cover six feet of wall. The wall was almost twelve feet wide and so I had to project the image in two segments and get them to meet up perfectly.

SPECIAL TOOLS
& MATERIALS

- Two stenciling rollers
- One ⅝" stencil brush
- White, medium gray, and light gray paint(these are the colors for the arbor only)
- Clear glaze
- Chalk pencil

See page 40 for details on
STANDARD TOOLS & MATERIALS

I suggest using either an overhead projector which can project your entire image, or the grid system. For a project as geometrical as this one, the grid system is a good choice because a projector will cause some distortion of your image at the extremities.

In the end, even though my husband had to wrestle the stenciling roller out of my hand twenty minutes before the guests arrived, the story had a happy ending. The wedding couldn't have been more perfect. The bride was radiant, the groom handsome, and the guests jovial. And for lasting memories, the photos were taken in a lovely garden room setting.

METHOD

1. To prepare the background wall, basecoat the wall using white paint with an eggshell or satin finish.

2. To create a soft early evening sky, use blue, yellow, and pink glazes. The glazes should be mixed using one part paint to four parts glaze (we use a glaze that contains an extender). Use painter's tape to tape off the walls adjacent to the mural and then, starting at the ceiling, use a large 4" high density foam roller to apply a thin coat of blue glaze. Immediately below this, roll on a thin coat of yellow glaze with a second roller. Then roll your roller back and forth many times where the colors meet so that one color melts into the other. If you wish to add clouds, as I did, use a large stenciling brush dipped in white paint. Remove the excess paint on a paper towel and add clouds using a pouncing motion. Create foreground clouds by pouncing with a freshly loaded brush. As the brush gets drier, the clouds will become fainter, and the background clouds will be formed.

3. For the background of trees, you can use the line drawing of this ridge as a guideline. Use a chalk pencil on your wall to indicate the ridge of trees. Use low-tack painter's tape to define the bottom of the trees from the start of the foreground field. Use large stencil brushes with a dry brush technique to pounce on the muted hues. I used various greens, yellow, and burgundy. Once these trees have dried, use your chalk pencil to outline the placement of the lower ridge of trees. Again, use stencil brushes and muted hues and a pouncing action to paint the trees. This ridge should be less muted than the background ridge.

4. Paint the field using various washes (one part paint, one part glaze, and three parts water), using blue-green, yellow-green, and yellow. Apply the washes at random, using a 2½" painter's brush. Use rapid, horizontal brush strokes to keep the washes from running.

5. Use the tree pattern provided in the West

Coast Scene and project it onto the wall to create the trees.

6. Cover the prepared wall with freezer paper and project the arbor onto the paper. Trace the arbor.

7. Cut out the medium gray shadow areas (the underside of the arbor) and roller stencil the exposed areas medium gray. Replace the cutouts once the paint dries. You may wish to use a hairdryer to speed up the process.

8. Roller stencil the other parts of the arbor white, making sure to cut out the pieces one segment at a time so appropriate shading may be added as necessary. Replace each cutout as soon as you finish stenciling it, as it may be needed to protect the area while you are shading the next area. Refer to photograph to see where to add your shading. Shade using the dry brush technique. We used medium gray paint mixed with glaze in a 1:1 ratio for shading.

9. Stencil both the front and the side view of the upright supporting posts in white. You may wish to stencil the front view a very pale gray to differentiate it from the side view, or you may wish to differentiate the front from the side view by drawing a line with a pencil and a straight edge between the two.

FOREGROUND PREPARATION

1. The stencils in the foreground are from the Buckingham Collection. We used ironwork, ivy border, leafy branch, clematis leaf (used in repetition to create a topiary), terra-cotta pots, flower pot, fern, iris, and blossom stencils. If you wish to make some of your own stencils, we have supplied line drawings you can project onto the wall. Apply the stencils using the "free form" method of stenciling. Free form stenciling means using a simple stencil over and over to build up realistic-looking images. This method of layering stencils creates a trompe l'oeil look. It is most successful if you vary colors and intensities between successive layers of prints. For instance, to stencil greenery, stencil your first layer (the background prints) a lighter and bluer hue than subsequent layers. Add glaze to your paint to make it more transparent and less intense, or use a paint that is more muted than the layers to follow. As you work into the foreground, your stencil repeats should appear brighter and bolder. Add detail to your foreground layer by using a stencil brush to blend in multicolored detail or shade around the edges of the leaves.

Pergola

◄ **139**

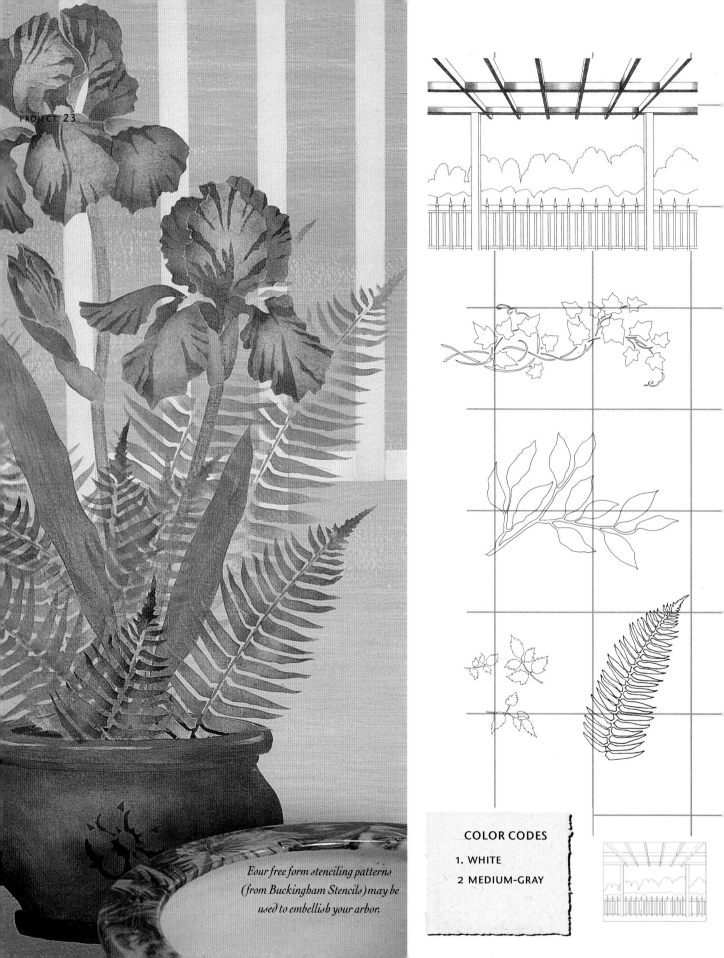

*Four free form stenciling patterns
(from Buckingham Stencils) may be
used to embellish your arbor.*

COLOR CODES

1. WHITE

2 MEDIUM-GRAY

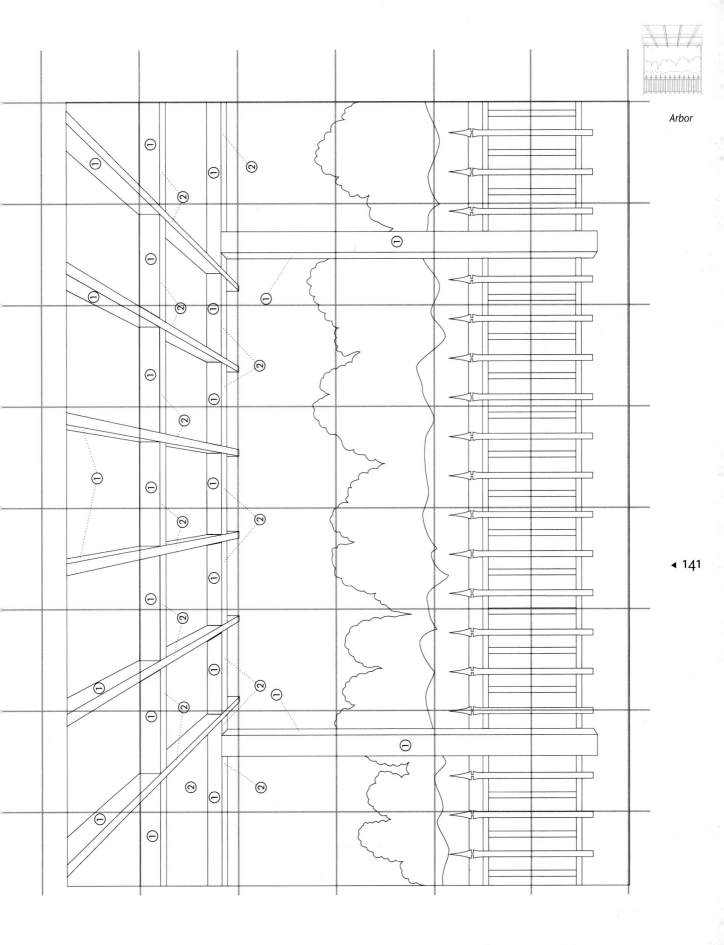

Arbor

Tropical Escape

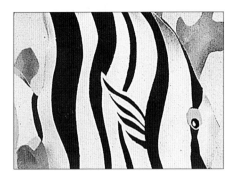

Leslie and I began our first business partnership when we were thirteen. I got the idea to start a lawn mowing business. Together we made up business cards and aggressively distributed them throughout the neighborhood. *Lawn mowing and trimming. 25 cents front. 50 cents front and back. Call Willow 1046 and ask for Linda.* The most obvious flaw in the plan was our lack of a lawnmower. Leslie's dad had a power mower which he said was too dangerous for us to use, and my dad wouldn't let us use his push mower, saying if we were going into business we needed our own. We ended up renting a push mower from a friend for 15 cents (I am sure her dad didn't know), but this amount cut seriously into our profits. The day after we distributed our cards, the phone started ringing. It was only then that I discovered my business partner was much smarter than I. She left that day to go on summer vacation with her family.

Leslie still prefers to go on vacation when it comes time to work, only now she escapes into fantasy holidays as part of her work. Leslie paints tropical fish and coral, while I paint salmon and penguins. While I stencil a West Coast scene with fir trees, cool morning mists, fishing boats, herons, and eagles, Leslie stencils sunny scenes with palm trees, cruise ships, beach sand, banana leaves, lizards, and coyotes.

SPECIAL TOOLS & MATERIALS

- Three stencil rollers (or one roller with several refills)
- Five stencil brushes in a variety of sizes
- White, pink, orange, purple, yellow, cobalt blue, yellow-green, and black paint, and pale blue low-luster latex house paint for the sea

See page 40 for details on
STANDARD TOOLS & MATERIALS

METHOD

1. Cut along the wavy water line, then remove the large piece that contains your underwater tropical scene.

2. Paint this entire area a light blue. Refer to the whale project for doing the sea with glazes. Shade a darker sea blue along the edge of your freezer paper pattern to emphasize the wavy water line.

3. Let the paint dry overnight before replacing the freezer paper with your pattern on it.

4. Begin by cutting out the coral. These pieces are marked as orange on your diagram. Save any coral cutouts that are touching the fish. Using a stencil roller, paint a base coat of pink in these cutout areas. Using a 1" stencil brush for each color and a pouncing action, randomly add in white and orange giving a mottled look. Once dry reposition the saved coral pieces. You may wish to speed up the drying process by using a hairdryer.

5. Stencil the orange and white fish next. Cut around their entire bodies, then remove and save the cutouts. Using a stencil roller, stencil these fish shapes white. You will need several coats of white to give you the opacity you want. Dry between coats and then replace these cutouts.

6. The orange sections are done next, one piece at a time, starting at the head and working backward. Cut out their heads first, then remove and save the cutouts. Using a stencil roller or a large 1" stencil brush, stencil these areas orange. When dry, shade dark orange (mix one part black to three parts orange) at back of the heads. Use a ½" stencil brush. Replace the head section and cut out the fish's eye. Paint it black with a small stencil brush. Next cut out the two middle sections (leaving the fins untouched) and stencil these areas orange, and shade them with the dark orange around the edges. Let the paint dry. Replace these middle body sections.

7. Cut out, remove, and discard the five fins and the tail. Using the same 1" stencil brush stencil these areas orange. Let the paint dry. With a stencil brush, shade the ends of the tail dark orange.

8. The yellow and blue fish are done next. Cut around the entire fish shape, save these cutouts, and roller stencil these fish white. Let the paint dry. Then paint these same areas a bright yellow. Let paint dry. Replace these cutouts.

9. Cut out the dark orange fins, remove these cutouts, and stencil them a dark orange using a stencil brush. Let the paint dry and replace all but the dark orange tail piece.

10. Cut out the cobalt blue stripes next. Remove the cutouts and discard all except for the stripe with the eye in it. Using a brush, stencil these areas cobalt blue. Replace the stripe piece containing the eye when the blue paint is dry. Cut out the eye and stencil it black. Place a small white dot inside the black eye.

11. The purple and white fish is done next. Cut out around the entire fish, then remove and save this piece. Using a stencil roller, paint this area white. Several coats will be necessary. Let the paint dry and shade a light purple (mix some purple into your white) around the outer edge to give the fish some three-dimensional shape. Replace this piece.

12. Cut out all the purple pieces. Discard all except for the stripe with the eye in it. Using a large 1" stencil brush, stencil these areas purple. Replaced saved stripe.

13. Cut out the three yellow pieces. These include the lips, the tip of the tail, and the eye. Using a ½" stencil brush stencil these areas yellow. Let the paint dry and replace the eye section. Cut out the pupil of the eye and stencil it black. Add a white highlight to the eye. When dry, dip the end of a small brush into some white paint and dot it on the eye.

14. The many small fish are next. Cut around their entire shapes, remove, and discard. Using a stencil roller, stencil these cutouts white. Let the paint dry. Pounce a variety of colors using a different ⅝" stencil brush for each color. We've used purple, fading into cobalt blue, fading into yellow green. While the paint was still soft, a sharp utility knife was used to lightly scratch into the surface paint to reveal the white paint underneath representing the gills and fin detail. This technique is called *"sgraffitto."* Place a small black dot in the fishes' eyes.

15. Remove all the freezer paper. After cutting out all those fish parts, you may be feeling like a fish monger but the result is worth the effort.

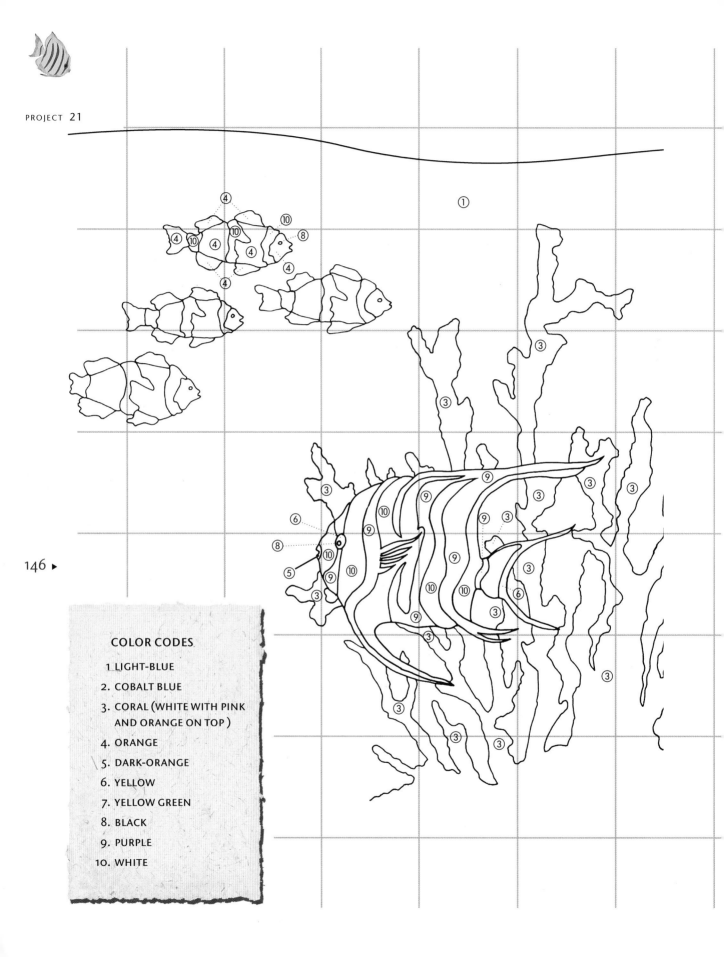

146 ▶

COLOR CODES

1. LIGHT-BLUE
2. COBALT BLUE
3. CORAL (WHITE WITH PINK AND ORANGE ON TOP)
4. ORANGE
5. DARK-ORANGE
6. YELLOW
7. YELLOW GREEN
8. BLACK
9. PURPLE
10. WHITE

Cypress Tree

Stained glass patterns are a good source of designs for projection stenciling. Years ago Leslie handcrafted the stained glass sun catcher pictured here in the background. She used a similar design to stencil this cypress mural, which looks very much at home in her West Coast contemporary surroundings.

METHOD

1. Make certain that the waterline is horizontal on your wall before you start cutting.

2. Cut out and remove the ring containing both the mortar and bricks and roller stencil it gray. Save this cutout. An uneven application of the paint will give the gray mortar a more realistic effect. If your paint bleeds a little under the freezer paper, don't worry, for this is one time the bleeding will actually improve your image since mortar is never completely smooth. Let the paint dry.

3. Reposition the ring.

4. Remove the large inner circle and stencil it white using a stencil roller. Save this cutout. Let paint dry. You can hasten the drying process by using a hairdryer.

5. Reposition the inner circle.

6. Cut out the entire sky area in one piece by following the tops of the mountains, the waterline, and along the bottom of the tree foliage where it intersects the mountain and follow the dotted line through

SPECIAL TOOLS & MATERIALS

- Six stencil brushes in a variety of sizes
- Four stencil rollers, or one stencil roller and three roller refills
- Acrylic varathane (gloss)
- Gray, light blue, medium blue, beige, dark beige, white, gray-purple, terra-cotta, light green, brown, black, red-brown, and dark green paint

See page 40 for details on
STANDARD TOOLS & MATERIALS

the tree (see the pattern). Save the cutout.

7. Stencil the sky a light blue using a stencil roller. With a large stencil brush pounce in billowy white clouds.

8. Let the sky dry and reposition its cutout.

9. Cut out the mountains and save the cutouts.

10. Using a roller, stencil the mountains a muted gray-purple.

11. Let the mountains dry and reposition the cutouts. Cut along the line that separates the mountain ranges. Use this edge to shade the left end of the foreground range.

12. Cut out the water. Save the cutouts. Stencil the water a medium blue using a stencil roller. Consider adding glaze to your blue to make it more translucent. Refer to whale project for a more elaborate sea treatment. *Note:* A glaze mixture will take longer to dry than a paint.

13. Let the water dry and reposition its cutouts.

14. Cut out the rock sections and stencil these with a brush one at a time. Save the cutouts. Stencil the rocks beige, shading dark beige around the outside edge of each one. Reposition each rock cutout before stenciling the adjacent rock cutout. Continue until all the rocks are stenciled and shaded.

15. Cut out the terra-cotta branches and terra-cotta trunk of the tree. Save the cutouts. Stencil these areas using brushes. Let paint dry.

16. Reposition the cutouts.

17. Cut out the brown branches and brown trunk of the tree. Save the cutouts. Three brown sections at the base of the tree trunk and two brown branch sections touch each other. These need to be cut out and stenciled one section at a time and shaded a dark brown (add a few drops of black to brown) around their outside edges so that they will stand out from each other. Reposition the cutouts as you go.

18. Cut out the light green foliage of the tree. Save the cutouts. Stencil these cutout areas light green and medium green using a large 1" stencil brush and a pouncing technique. Let the paint dry, and reposition the cutouts as you go.

19. Cut out the dark green foliage. Use a large 1" stencil brush and a pouncing technique to stencil them dark and medium green.

20. Cut out all the bricks. To create the multi-colored brick look, load three stencil brushes, one with black paint, one with red-brown, and one with white. In each cutout pounce in all three colors randomly. To finish off the mural, roller stencil a gloss water-based varathane over the entire scene, excluding the ring of bricks. This will make it seem as though the viewer is looking at the scene through glass, by making that part of the mural glossier than the rest. *Note:* Wait several days before applying the varathane.

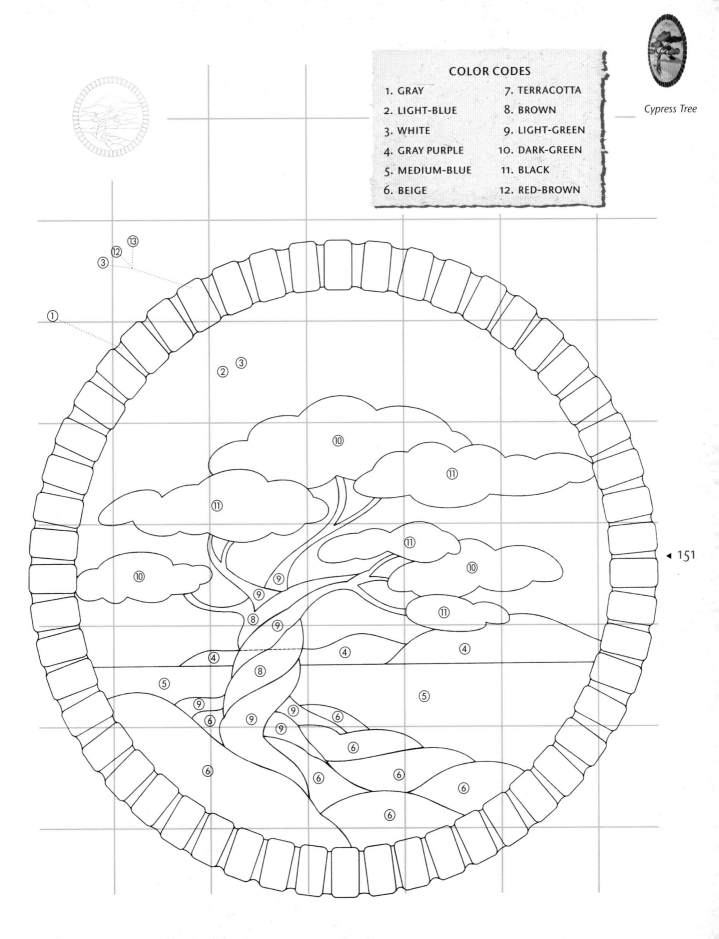

COLOR CODES

1. GRAY
2. LIGHT-BLUE
3. WHITE
4. GRAY PURPLE
5. MEDIUM-BLUE
6. BEIGE
7. TERRACOTTA
8. BROWN
9. LIGHT-GREEN
10. DARK-GREEN
11. BLACK
12. RED-BROWN

Cypress Tree

◀ 151

Cottage Window

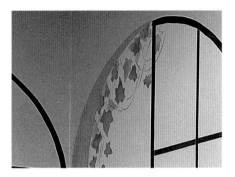

"I really like your purple bath and sink. It's a good thing you didn't replace them as most people do," remarked my neighbor, Maribel.

The truth is that neither my husband nor I could stand the purple bathroom fixtures when we first bought our house. To us they were a reminder of the worst decor of the '60s—shag carpeting, avocado kitchen appliances, and orange bath sets. But given the cost of replacing them, we decided to live with our dislike. Recently I color-washed the walls of the ensuite a soft gold (the complementary color of purple) and then stenciled a cottage window with a garden view featuring purple foxgloves. Suddenly our outdated sink and bathtub seemed just right!

METHOD

1. Cut out the exterior window opening following the dotted line and the left side of the black window frame. See the illustration. Save this cutout.

2. If your wall is not white, roller stencil the opening white. It will probably take several coats to achieve smooth, uniform coverage.

3. Now comes the fun part or the intimidating part, depending on your sense of adventure. Play with various glazes, paints, and stencils to

create your own fantasy window on the world. We used a sky blue glaze as the background and then we used a large stencil brush to pounce on background greenery in very muted tones. This gives the illusion of a misty summer morning, and hides the fact that we aren't skilled artists! Several repeats of the foxglove stencil (from Buckingham Stencils) were used to fill in the foreground. We used the ivy stencil (from Buckingham) around the rim of the opening. See Project 20 for several botanical stencils you can enlarge.

4. Now replace the opening cutout.

5. Cut out the side window casing and roller stencil this a darker shade than your wall color. Replace the cutout when the paint has dried.

6. Cut out the windowsill. Roller stencil this area a lighter shade than your wall. If your wall is white, you do not need to stencil this cutout. Replace the cutout.

7. Cut out both window frames and latch, and stencil these areas black. For a more realistic-looking latch, cut out one component at a time and replace before cutting out and stenciling the next component.

8. Remove all the freezer paper.

9. Using painter's tape, mask off the inside edge of the windowsill. With a stenciling brush, shade along the edge of the tape to further define the sill from the wall. If your wall and sill are both white, this step is crucial, for without it, there would be no definition between the two.

10. The flower pot and primroses are from Buckingham Stencils and have been stenciled on the window sill to increase the illusion. There's no fear of this pot falling out the window!

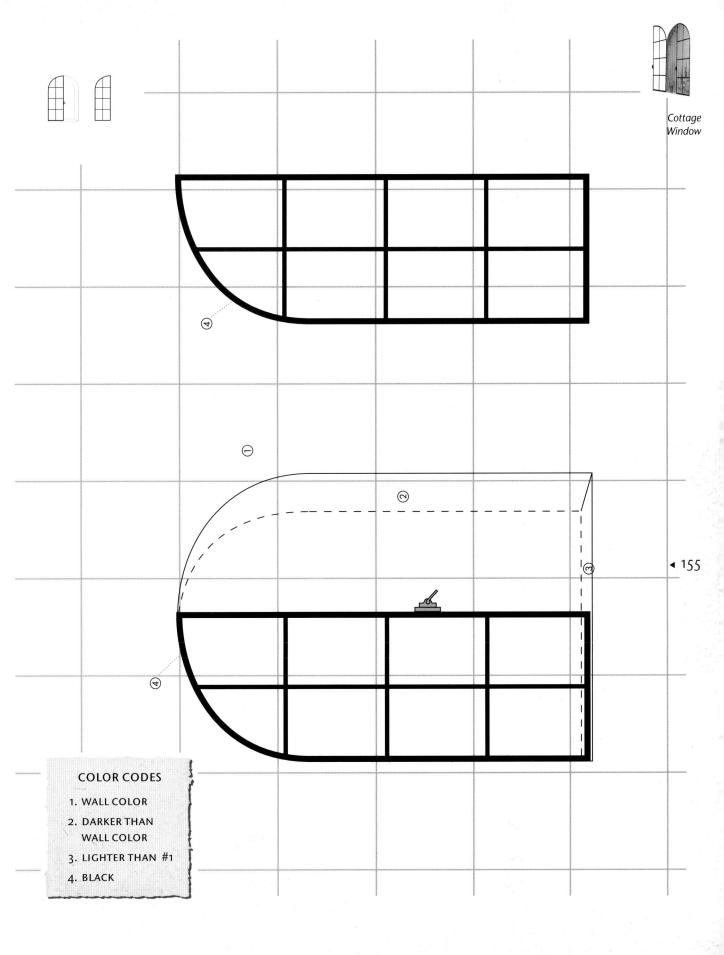

Cottage
Window

◄ 155

COLOR CODES

1. WALL COLOR
2. DARKER THAN
   WALL COLOR
3. LIGHTER THAN #1
4. BLACK

PART V

Stencil the World

Years ago I discovered this wonderful heading tucked away in the operating expense column on my company's profit and loss statement: R & D. Research and development. Those two little words have opened up a whole new world to me. In this section of the book we show stenciling inspired by artwork and landscapes from Mexico, Southwest Africa, Arizona, the west coast of Canada, and Greece. It seems to me that we might also need stencils of the Orient, Australia, New Zealand, and the Galapagos. I'll tuck sunscreen into my luggage, look up at my husband, and say with a smile, "Don't worry, dear. It's all business. You know—research and development. Somebody has to do it."

Greek Isle Scene
A Shirley Valentine Room

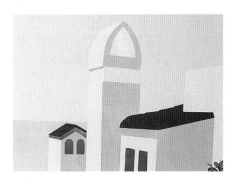

"A Shirley Valentine Room," our friend, Chris, replied when we asked her what she had in mind as a decorating theme for her sewing room. She was referring to the British movie, *Shirley Valentine*, in which a bored housewife's life is rekindled when she throws caution to the winds, and gambles on romance in the Greek Islands. The opening scene of the movie shows a discontented, middle-aged Shirley talking to the kitchen wall in her working-class row house while she cooks eggs and chips for her husband.

We stenciled a serene Greek Island scene for Chris to capture the spirit of the movie and to remind her of the movie's message, which is that it is never too late to realize your dreams. And, if Chris is inclined to talk to walls, what a fine one in which to confide!

METHOD

1. Using a sharp X-acto® knife, cut out the window opening and save the cutout (do not cut out the window ledge or casing). Run your fingers carefully around the cut edges to make sure they are affixed to the wall.

2. If your wall is not white, roller stencil this opening white, making sure to use the dry roller technique along the edges of the freezer paper so the paint doesn't bleed under the paper. It will probably take several coats of paint to get adequate coverage. You may want to use

◀ 159

SPECIAL TOOLS & MATERIALS

- Five stenciling rollers (or one stencil roller and four refills)
- One ¾" stencil brush
- Water-based glaze
- White, dark cyan blue, cyan blue, light cyan blue, deep red, light gray, medium gray, and dark-gray paint

See page 40 for details on
STANDARD TOOLS & MATERIALS

a hairdryer to speed up the drying process. Once the white paint is dry, replace the cutout.

3. Cut out the sky by cutting along the horizon and around the tops of the buildings.

4. Give the background sky a translucent finish using water-based glazes. Mix a cyan blue glaze by adding one part cyan blue paint to four parts glaze and then mix a lighter cyan blue. With a stenciling roller, roll on a thin coat of cyan blue glaze and then a thin coat of the lighter cyan blue glaze below it. Roll the roller back and forth several times where the colors meet so that one color melts into the other. Work quickly with glazes to avoid lap lines in your finish. If you wish to make this step easier, you can paint your sky rather than glaze it.

5. If you used glaze for your sky, take a break at this point and allow the sky to dry. Glazes take quite a bit longer to dry than paints. Once again, a hairdryer will speed up the process. Once the sky is dry, replace its cutout.

6. Finish cutting out the sea by cutting around the building and, using a stenciling roller, apply a thin coat of dark cyan blue (one part paint to four parts glaze) and then a thin coat of cyan blue glaze below the dark cyan blue. See Step #5 for blending one color into the next. If you wish to make this step easier, you may want to use paint rather than glazes for your sea.

When the glaze or paint is dry, replace the sea cutout.

7. Cut out, stencil, and replace the cutouts for the light gray and medium gray sections. Do these cutouts one at a time, let each one dry, and replace their pieces before proceeding to the next.

8. Cut out and stencil the dark-gray and deep red sections.

9. Cut out the side window casing and roller stencil this area a darker shade than your wall. If your wall is white, stencil this area light gray. When the paint is dry, replace the cutout.

10. Cut out the windowsill. Stencil it a lighter tint than the wall color. If your wall is white, you do not need to stencil this cutout. When the paint is dry, replace the cutout.

11. If your wall is white, use painter's tape to mask off the windowsill. With a stenciling brush, lightly shade along the edge to define the sill from the wall.

12. There are several places on this mural where the white top of the railing disappears into the white of walls. To define these areas, we drew a pencil line with a ruler to separate them.

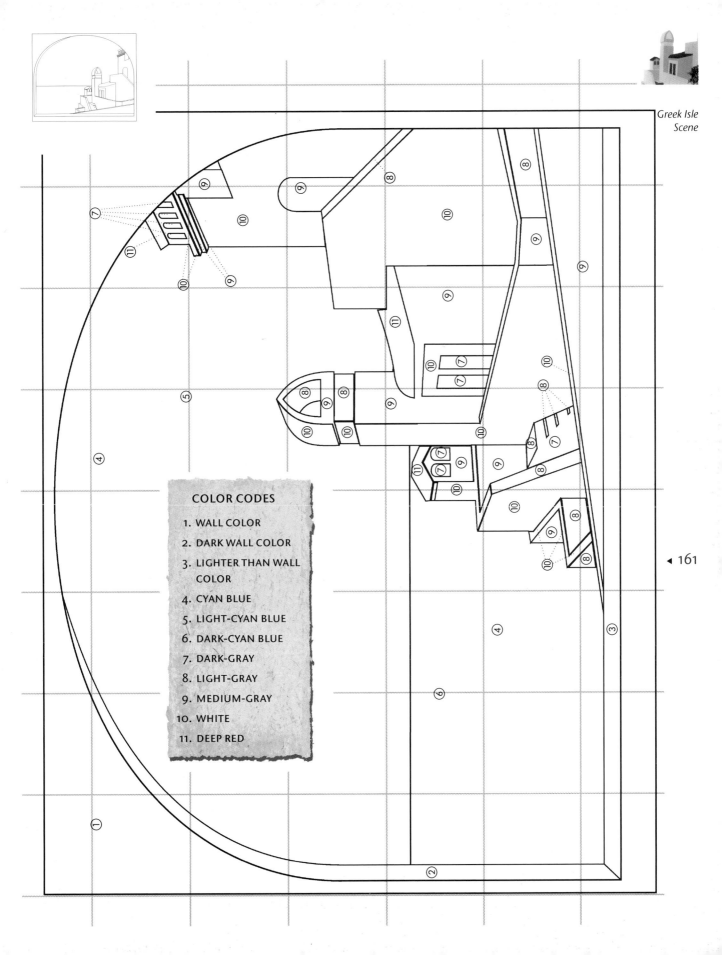

COLOR CODES

1. WALL COLOR
2. DARK WALL COLOR
3. LIGHTER THAN WALL COLOR
4. CYAN BLUE
5. LIGHT-CYAN BLUE
6. DARK-CYAN BLUE
7. DARK-GRAY
8. LIGHT-GRAY
9. MEDIUM-GRAY
10. WHITE
11. DEEP RED

◄ 161

Delicado's
FIESTA
74-40
TOMATO FILETS
MEYER
GROS FLOCONS
AVOINE (IRIS)

Arizona Desert

SPECIAL TOOLS & MATERIALS

For Scene 1, Arizona Desert
- Three stencil rollers (or one roller and two refills)
- Three 1" stencil brushes
- White, golden yellow, orange, medium green, light green, dark green, and black paint

For Scene 2, the Painted Desert
- Five stencil rollers (or one roller and four refills)
- Two stencil brushes, ½" and ⅝"
- White, sky blue, light gray, dark gray, terra-cotta, and dark brown paint

See page 40 for details on
STANDARD TOOLS & MATERIALS

Georgene, the owner of Delicado's, wanted Leslie to paint a bright, bold, southwest mural on the back wall of her restaurant. Leslie loves to escape into a fantasy world when she stencils, so this assignment was right up her alley. But this time, as she painted the upper reaches of the mural, Leslie began to fear she had gone too far into her daydreaming. She was standing on top of a large commercial freezer when she began to feel a hot breeze rise up as if from the desert below!

Although this mural was painted in a restaurant, it could just as easily find a home on a wall behind a wet bar, in a games room, in a kitchen nook, or a child's bedroom (as a backdrop to a rocking horse).

METHOD

1. Cut out the sun by cutting along the hill line and following the dotted line at the base of the coyote. Save this cutout.
2. Stencil the sun golden yellow using a stencil roller. If your wall is a dark color stencil the sun with a white base coat before stenciling the yellow. This may require several coats.
3. Shade around the outer rim of the sun with the orange. If you mix in some glaze with the orange paint it will give a more translucent look and a smoother blending of colors.

4. Reposition the sun cutout.

5. Cut out the coyote and the hills and discard the cutout. Stencil this black with a stencil roller. You will need several coats to give it a solid appearance.

6. The cactus is a little more involved. Cut out the main stock and save the cutout. Stencil it a medium green. If you are stenciling on a dark color you should stencil this white before stenciling it green.

7. With a large stencil brush shade the side of the cactus a dark green. See the photograph as a guide.

8. Highlight the near side of the cactus with a light green. Add a touch of yellow and orange with a pouncing action to give this area a golden glow, as if it were reflecting the sunlight.

9. Reposition the main cactus stock cutout.

10. Cut out the thin vertical lines on the main stock. Stencil these a dark green.

11. Cut the limbs and save the cutouts.

12. Stencil the limbs medium green. (If stenciling on a dark color stencil this section white first.)

13. Shade the sides of the limbs with a dark green (refer to photograph).

14. Highlight the near side of the right limbs with light green. Pounce on a touch of yellow and rust for a golden glow.

15. Reposition the limb cutouts.

16. Cut out the vertical lines on the limbs. Stencil these a dark green.

17. Remove all the freezer paper and stencil on the prickly spines with the stencil line drawing provided. Photocopy these patterns. Cut this stencil out of clear acetate or mylar rather than freezer paper. This will allow you to see through the stencil for accurate placement. Stencil these "V"s and "1"s randomly along the outside edge of the cactus and down the vertical lines inside the cactus.

Don't limit yourself to just one cactus—cut several different sizes and change the appearance by reversing the stencil design when you enlarge them.

THE PAINTED DESERT

This scene is only one of an infinite number of vistas that you can create for any room in your home. Because we live a rain belt, hot desert scenes on a wall help get one through long dreary winters. As well, many of our landscape images can be adjusted to fit into this arched window shape.

METHOD

Refer to steps 1–3 of Project 24 for the Greek Isle scene.

1. Cut out the sky by cutting along the top of the clouds and around the glider. Remove and save the sky piece. The glider piece will remain in position until it is stenciled.

2. Using a stencil roller, stencil the sky a light blue. Several coats of paint may be necessary. Let paint dry and reposition the sky piece.

3. The cumulus clouds are cut out next. They are cut out one at a time and saved.

Working from your left to your right, cut out and remove the first cloud. With a small ½" stencil, shade the right-hand side of the cloud a light gray. (This just involves a shading to differentiate one cloud from the one adjacent to it.) Replace this cutout and proceed to the next cloud until all have been shaded on the right and replaced.

4. Cut out the entire landform section. This should be one large piece. Remove and save this piece. Paint this area a terra-cotta using a stencil roller. Let the paint dry and reposition this piece.

5. Cut out all the pieces indicated as dark brown, remove, and discard. Using a roller, stencil this area a dark brown.

6. Remove the glider cutout next, save this piece, and using your light gray stencil brush, basecoat the cutout area a light gray. Let the paint dry and reposition this cutout.

7. Lastly, cut out the dark gray sections of the glider and discard them. Using a stencil brush, stencil these a dark gray.

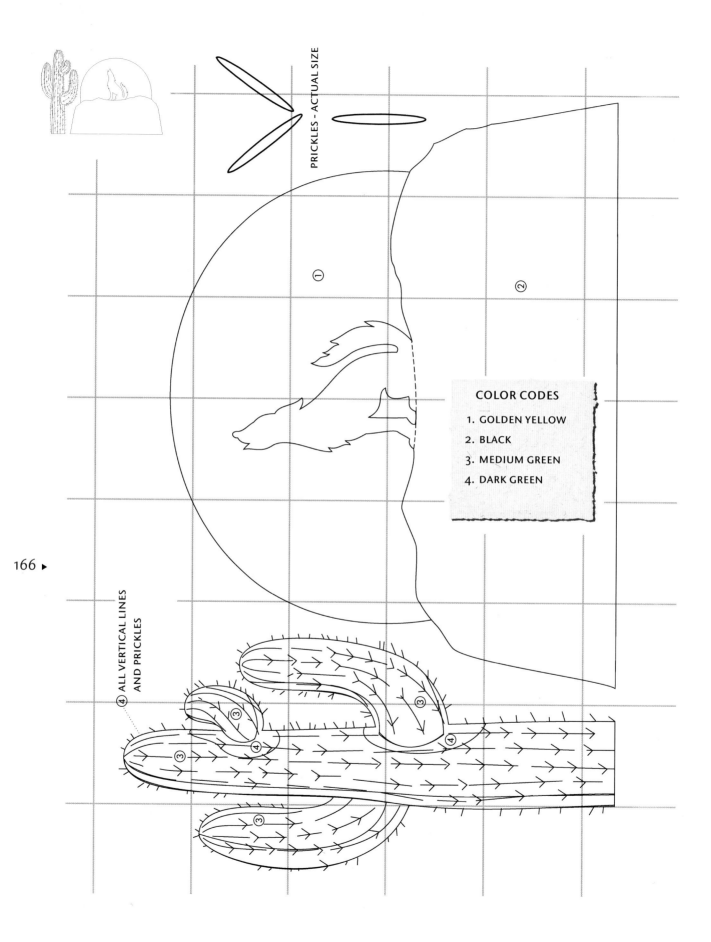

PRICKLES - ACTUAL SIZE

COLOR CODES

1. GOLDEN YELLOW
2. BLACK
3. MEDIUM GREEN
4. DARK GREEN

ALL VERTICAL LINES AND PRICKLES

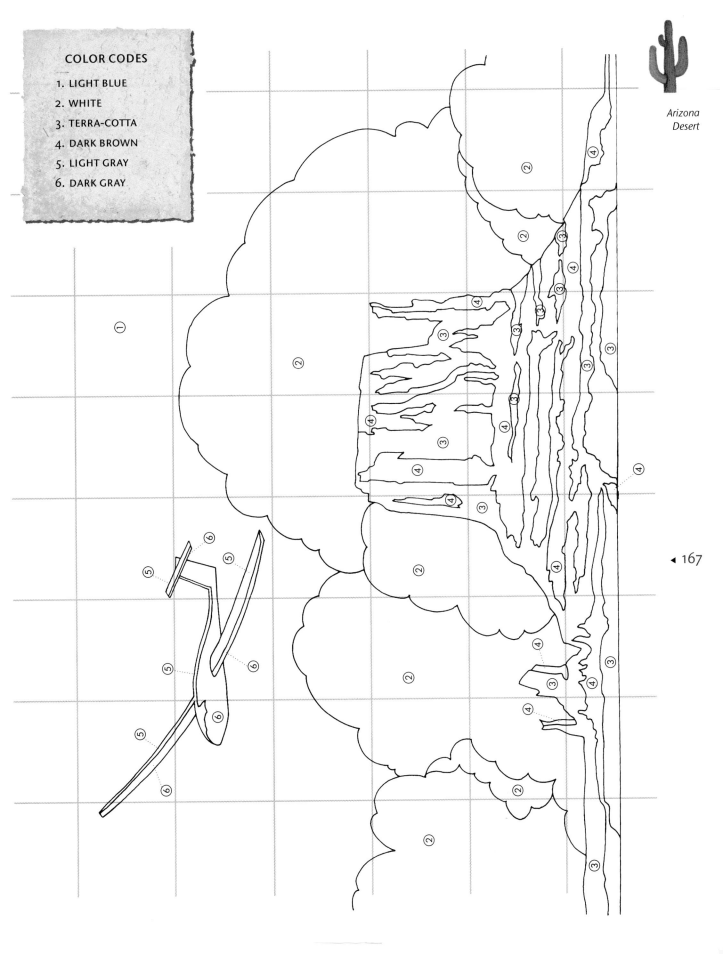

COLOR CODES

1. LIGHT BLUE
2. WHITE
3. TERRA-COTTA
4. DARK BROWN
5. LIGHT GRAY
6. DARK GRAY

Arizona Desert

◄ 167

West Coast Scene

*I*magine waking up and gazing out the window onto a West Coast seascape shaking off its early morning mist. And the price of this exquisite real estate? All it cost us was a few hours of time! We found the folding closet doors in a neighbor's garbage, gave them a light sanding, primed them, and then used our projection stenciling technique to create a room with a view.

METHOD

1. Cut out the sky section of the freezer paper, cutting through the top of the fir tree in the process. Save the piece of freezer paper.

2. To give the background sky a subtle finish, use water-based glazes. Mix a pink glaze by adding one part pink paint to four parts glaze, and mix a yellow glaze by adding one part yellow paint to four parts glaze. Using a stenciling roller, roll on a thin coat of pink glaze and then a thin coat of yellow glaze below the pink. Move the roller back and forth many times where the colors meet so that one color melts into the other and you can't tell where one ends and the next begins. Remember that it is important to work quickly with glazes to avoid lap lines in your finish. Also, glaze mixtures dry more slowly than paint, so allow plenty of drying time. You may wish to use a hairdryer to speed up the drying time. A simpler alternative to using glazes is to fill in the sky with one color using paint. Be sure to use a dry

SPECIAL TOOLS & MATERIALS

- Five stencil rollers
- One 1" stencil brush
- Water-based glaze
- Mountain green, forest green, black-green, pink, white, yellow, and mauve paint

See page 40 for details on
STANDARD TOOLS & MATERIALS

stenciling technique around the edges of the freezer paper. Once the paint is dry, replace the sky cutout.

3. Cut out the distant mountains and roller stencil them mauve. Again, you will be cutting through the fir tree as you cut out this mountain range. Several coats of paint may be needed. Use a dry roller technique as you near edges to prevent paint from bleeding under the freezer paper.

4. Use a very dry brush stenciling technique with white paint to pounce in mist at the base of the mountains. Once the paint is dry, replace the mountain cutout.

5. Cut out the closer mountain range, the one behind the two islands, and save the cutout piece. As you cut along the tops of the two islands and along the water-line, again cut through the fir tree. Using a roller, stencil this mountain range soft mountain green. Again, pounce in mist at the base of the mountains. Replace cutout once paint drys.

6. Cut out the two island pieces and save the cutouts. Once again, cut through the fir tree. By now you are probably beginning to feel like a logger, but don't worry. You get to start your reforestation once all the tree-bearing sections have been replaced. Stencil the

islands dark green. When the paint is dry, replace the cutouts.

7. Cut out the water and set the piece aside. Roll on glazes (or paint, if you prefer) as you did for the sky, reversing the colors with yellow above the pink. This technique will make the sky appear to be reflected in the water. Replace the water cutout once the "water" is dry. If you used glaze for your sea, allow plenty of drying time (at least overnight).

8. Cut out the foreground bushes and tree and discard their cutouts. Roller stencil these areas black-green. Several coats of paint will be necessary.

9. Remove all the remaining freezer paper.

10. Stand back and admire the view!

Note: This is a great scene for closet doors. Doors are subjected to a lot of wear and tear so you may want to protect your masterpiece with a coat of acrylic varnish. Be sure to allow your stencils to dry for a few days before applying the varnish.

COLOR CODES

1. PALE PINK
2. PALE YELLOW
3. MAUVE
4. MOUNTAIN GREEN
5. DARK GREEN
6. BLACK GREEN

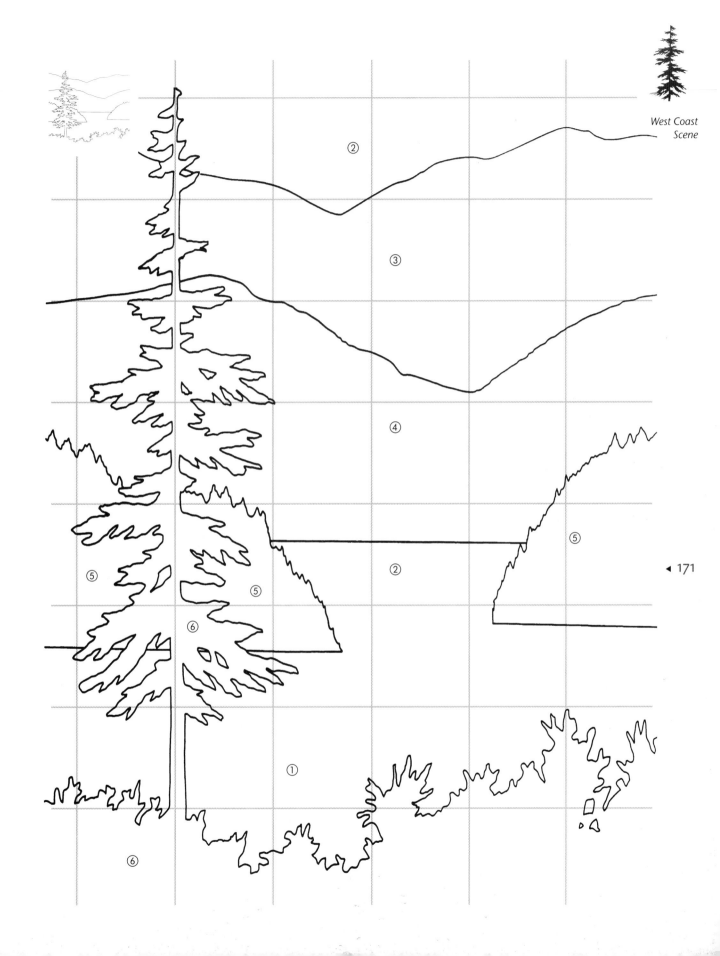

West Coast Scene

◀ 171

African Cave Art Figures
&
Mexican Design on Sisal

Leslie and I have different stenciling techniques. I have a light touch and Leslie, by my estimation, is slightly more heavy-handed. This is one project where Leslie's heavy-handedness paid dividends. Sisal really soaks up paint, so very little down-loading (getting rid of excess paint) is necessary when stenciling on sisal. Leslie painted half the figures and I painted the other half. She was done much faster than I was because I had to give my figures a second coat. Even though the surface of sisal is very uneven, you will be surprised at how clean your edges appear. Make sure you use a pouncing stenciling technique rather than a swirling technique because the freezer paper does not adhere well to the sisal, and it will be more inclined to stay in place if you pounce rather than swirl.

The figures on the cave art carpet are taken from Bushman cave art in southwest Africa, and the gecko design is a traditional Mexican image.

◄ 173

SPECIAL TOOLS & MATERIALS

- One 1" stencil brush
- Clay red paint

See page 40 for details on
STANDARD TOOLS & MATERIALS

METHOD

1. Place your freezer paper on the wall and project your image onto it. Trace around the image and remove the paper.

2. Place the pattern on your sisal carpet. The coarser the fibers in the carpet, the less effective the spray adhesive will be for holding it firmly in position. You might find it easier to also tape the pattern in place using masking tape around the outside.

3. Carefully cut out one figure and discard the cutout. Using a large 1" stencil brush and a pouncing action, work the clay red paint into the carpet. Use less paint as you approach the edge of the freezer paper so your edges remain clean. For the Mexican design, just cut out and stencil the one pattern.

4. Cut out the next figure, paint, and proceed until all the figures are completed.

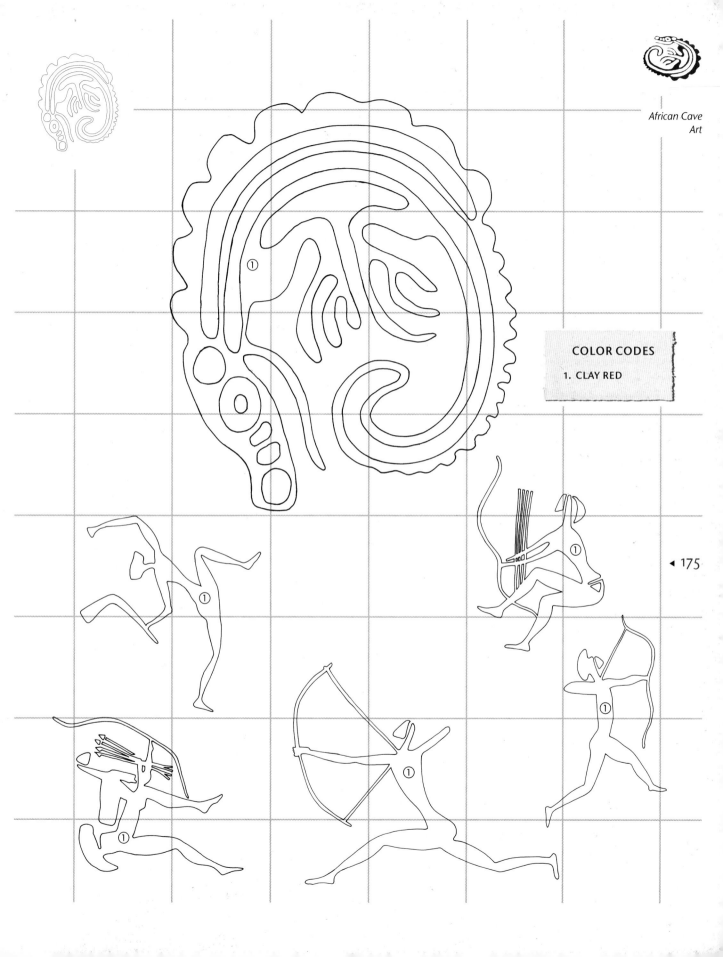

COLOR CODES

1. CLAY RED

◄ 175

Cruise Ship

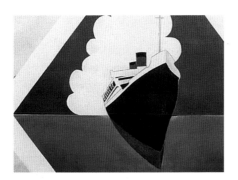

*Y*ou never know when your ship might come in. Late one evening at work, Leslie spied a dozen doors discarded in a pile with work "dunnage" written across them in a black marker. There, free for the taking, was the new door she needed for a stenciling project With projection stenciling you can change garage sale finds, relative's cast offs, factory seconds, and your own tired household belongings into works of art.

METHOD

1. Measure your door and cut a piece of freezer paper the corresponding size. Project and trace the design on the freezer paper.
2. Basecoat the entire door with low-luster white latex. You may need to prime your door first, depending on its finish.
3. Place the freezer paper pattern on your door. Cut carefully around the doorknob or remove it.
4. Paint the background scene first and the cruise ship insert later.
5. Start with the light blue background sky. Cut out and set aside the areas indicated as sky. *Note:* Cut around the mountains, along the sides of the white diamond, and through the palm tree trunks (as indicated by a dotted line on the color-coded diagram). Paint the sky area a mix of light blue, medium blue, and white. You can use a combination of

◄ 177

SPECIAL TOOLS & MATERIALS

- One stencil and four roller refills
- Four or five stencil brushes (assorted sizes)
- Low-luster white latex
- Dark blue, light blue, medium blue, midnight blue, light midnight blue, white, yellow-green, dark green, gray-green, light brown, medium brown, dark brown, maroon, gold, black, beige, and white paint

See page 40 for details on
STANDARD TOOLS & MATERIALS

stencil rollers to lay down the two blues and a 1" stencil brush for the white cloud streaks. Be careful to use a dry brush technique as you near the edge of the freezer paper to prevent paint from bleeding through. You can increase the "open" time of the paint by adding some glaze to your sky colors (add about one part paint to one part glaze). Work quickly to blend the colors before the paint has time to fully dry. You are trying to create a somewhat streaky look, so alternate the colors in bands. Let the paint dry, then replace the sky cutout piece.

6. Cut out the sea areas. Remove and set aside these pieces. Paint the sea medium blue with a few streaks of white running through it. Use a 1" stencil brush in a horizontal dragging action to

simulate the water. Let the paint dry and then replace the cutouts.

7. Cut out and remove the gray-green mountain pieces. Using a stencil roller, paint these areas gray-green. Let the paint dry and replace these pieces.

8. Cut the background sand out next and save the two cutout pieces. Cut out the larger of the sand pieces by cutting through the dotted lines shown on the color-coded pattern and then cutting around the bottom of the white border. Using a stencil roller, stencil the exposed area beige. Let the paint dry and replace the paper pieces.

9. Cut out and save the trunks of the palm trees. Using a stencil roller, paint these areas light brown, and let the paint dry. Shade the edges of the trunks dark brown using a ½" stencil brush. Replace the trunk cutouts.

10. Next, stencil the palm fronds. Cut out all the foreground palm fronds, saving all the pieces where one frond overlaps another. Stencil all the fronds yellow-green using a stencil roller. With a ½" stencil brush, shade the lower side of the fronds a darker green. Let the paint dry and replace the saved pieces. Now, cut out the remaining background fronds and save any pieces of frond that touch the trunks of the palm trees. Roller stencil the exposed areas dark green. (This isn't as complicated as it sounds. You are creating the illusion of depth by having

foreground and background fronds —light green in front and dark green in the background.)

11. Cut out the small slits in the trunks and stencil them white using a small ½" stencil brush. You can also paint these freehand if you wish.

12. To paint the coconuts, it will be easier if you cut a small separate stencil in the shape of a 1" oval and stencil clusters in dark brown (refer to photograph for placement).

13. Cut out the banana leaves, carefully cutting around the lizard. Remove these pieces and set them aside. Using a stencil roller, paint the exposed areas yellow-green. Let the paint dry and replace the cutouts. Cut out and set aside the areas designated as dark green. Roller stencil the exposed spaces dark green. Replace the cutouts.

14. Cut out the lizard and set the piece aside. Stencil the lizard medium brown using a ⅝" stencil brush and highlight with gold. Once the paint is dry, replace the cutout. Cut out the markings on the underbelly, eye, and tail. Using a ½" stencil brush stencil these openings dark brown.

15. Stencil the cruise ship section next. Cut out the sky first by cutting around the outside of the smoke, around the top of mast, and the port side of the ship. Remove the cutout and set it aside. Roller stencil the exposed area midnight blue. Let the paint dry and replace the cutout.

16. Cut out the ocean piece next by cutting around the hull of the ship, around the

banana leaf tip, and across the horizon. Add some white paint to your midnight blue to create a slightly lighter tone to distinguish it from your night sky. Let the paint dry and then replace this piece.

17. Cut out the black sections of the ship next, including the hull, the tops of the two smoke stacks, the windows, and the thin lines differentiating the white of the ship from the white of the smoke. Alternately, you may wish to draw these thin lines with a sharp pencil. Save the cutouts for the hull and the tops of the smoke stacks. Let the paint dry and replace the saved cutouts.

18. Cut out the mast at the front of the ship. Remove and discard this piece. Using a ½" stencil brush, stencil the exposed area gold.

19. Finally, cut out the maroon pieces and using a ⅝" stencil brush, stencil the exposed areas maroon. Remove all the freezer paper and wait for your ship to come in!

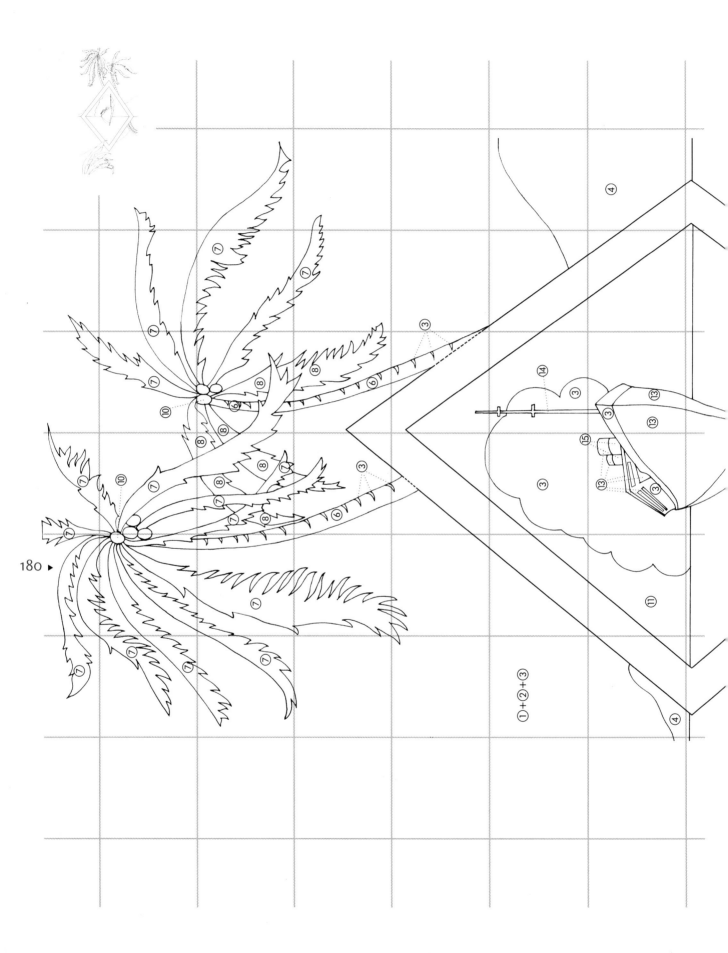

180 ▶

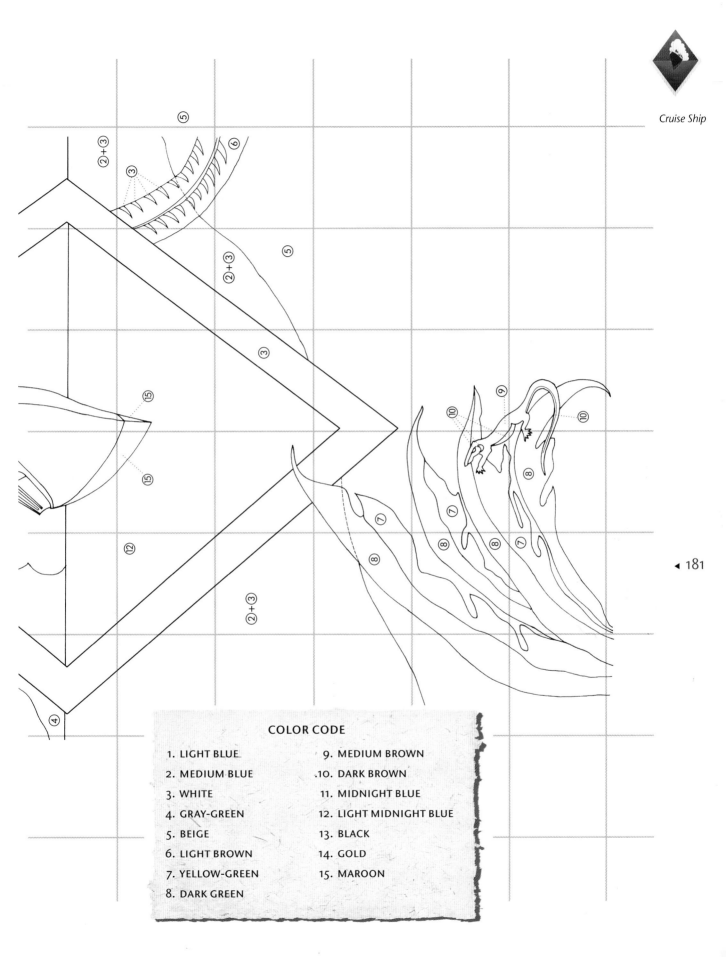

◄ 181

COLOR CODE

1. LIGHT BLUE
2. MEDIUM BLUE
3. WHITE
4. GRAY-GREEN
5. BEIGE
6. LIGHT BROWN
7. YELLOW-GREEN
8. DARK GREEN

9. MEDIUM BROWN
.10. DARK BROWN
11. MIDNIGHT BLUE
12. LIGHT MIDNIGHT BLUE
13. BLACK
14. GOLD
15. MAROON

PART VI

Faking It!

hy settle for the real thing when it is so much more fun to fake it? When people admire the wood inlay or glass etching on my boat I am quick to point out they are looking at stenciling. Always intrigued, they want to know more, so I embark on a detailed description of the stenciling process. My husband used to enjoy this discourse, but he has now heard it so many times that when friends make complimentary remarks, he wishes I would come back with a simple "Thank you." Not a chance!

Wood "Inlaid" Tabletop

SPECIAL TOOLS & MATERIALS

- Wooden object to stencil (We recommend a closed-grained wood such as maple or birch. Your object need not be made of solid wood. Veneer will do just as well.)
- Old Master's Gel Stains (any gel stain will work but you must check the compatibility of the stain with the protective clear coats)
- An assortment of stencil brushes
- Semigloss oil-based spray varathane
- 400 grit sandpaper

See page 40 for details on
STANDARD TOOLS & MATERIALS

I needed to have a table with folding legs so it could be stowed while we were at sea and would fit comfortably into the confined quarters of our boat. As I was going to all the bother of having it specially made, I thought to myself, "Why not stencil it?" I decided to use wood stains to mimic the look of inlaid wood rather than paints to stencil the table. Our boat has a rich interior of mahogany and teak and I thought faux inlaid wood would complement the décor.

I was not disappointed with the results. We all know you can fool some of the people all of the time and all of the people some of the time. But the big question was, could we fool Chris? Chris is a Swiss-trained master craftsman and the shipwright who was doing renovations on our boat at the time.

"So," I said to Chris at the first opportunity, "What do you think of our new table?"

"Well, it looks very fine."

"I did the design on the tabletop myself," I said, not too modestly.

"You?" he said, looking quite surprised, "How long did it take you?"

"Oh, about four hours."

"Don't you mean four days?" he corrected me, believing it to be authentic inlaid wood.

I couldn't have been happier!

The secret to creating faux inlaid wood is in using wood gel stains for your coloring agent, and in scoring the wood with your X-acto® knife when you cut out your design.

The projects shown here—coffee table, trays, and the cover of the photo album—were all stenciled using the same method.

METHOD

1. Prepare the wood surface by lightly sanding in the direction of the wood grain using very fine sandpaper.
2. Stain the entire surface of the wood with natural stain following the instructions on the gel stain tin. Allow the stain to dry overnight.
3. Draw or trace your design onto the shiny side of your freezer paper and affix the paper to your wood surface using repositionable stencil adhesive.
4. Using an X-acto® knife, cut out your design. Apply enough pressure to deeply score the wood in order to add to the illusion that the design is inlaid.
5. Peel off the sections of the design you wish to stain darker. Stencil these with gel stains, using a dry brush stenciling technique. For more intense color, allow the stain to dry overnight before adding another coat. The designs shown here were stenciled using natural, cherry, and dark mahogany stains.

6. Once the stain has dried, add several coats of semigloss varathane to the whole surface, being sure to allow each coat to dry before applying subsequent coats. Make sure you use spray varathane for at least your first coat. If you brush on your first coat of varathane your stains may run. Do not sand your first coat of varathane as it is easy to accidentally sand through your stains, but do sand lightly after subsequent coats with very fine sandpaper.

Wood Inlaid
Tabletop

◄ 187

COLOR CODES

1. MAHOGANY STAIN

2. CHERRY STAIN

3. NATURAL STAIN

For the pattern please see
page 187.

Wood "Inlaid" Fridge Panel

A Raven by Any Other Name

◄ 189

The featured artwork on our boat is *Dancing Spirit,* a print by native artist Lloyd Joseph. In choosing a design for our fridge panel I wanted to stay with the native theme, and decided to take on the challenge of coming up with my own design. After poring over volumes of Northwest Indian art books I was quite pleased to come up with the design pictured here. But when I asked Leslie how she liked my eagle, she said, "Eagle? That's not an eagle! It's a thunderbird. See the curlicue? That means it's a thunderbird."

Later in the day my son, Kirk, and his girlfriend, Lara, dropped by. I asked Lara, who is of native ancestry, what she thought of my thunderbird. She burst out laughing. "Thunderbird? That's not a thunderbird! It's a raven. See the moon in his mouth? It's the raven who carries the sun and the moon in his mouth to bring us day and night."

"That's not a moon," I replied a bit defensively, "It's a berry! I thought since the eagle was on a fridge, he should have some food in his mouth."

METHOD

See page 186.

SPECIAL TOOLS & MATERIALS

- Wooden object to stencil (We recommend a closed-grained wood such as maple or birch. Your object need not be made of solid wood. Veneer will do just as well.)
- Old Master's Gel Stains (any gel stain will work but you must check the compatibility of the stain with the protective clear coats)
- An assortment of stencil brushes
- Semigloss oil-based spray varathane
- 400 grit sandpaper

See page 40 for details on
STANDARD TOOLS & MATERIALS

Tiled Garden Table

SPECIAL TOOLS & MATERIALS

- Utility knife with at least five snap-off blades
- Painter's tape, 2" wide
- Three stencil rollers (or one roller and two refills)
- Four ⅝" stencil brushes
- Two standard 2" paint brushes
- Acrylic primer (exterior-grade), for basecoating tiles
- Sandpaper—120 grit
- Sky blue, dark blue, very light, medium, and dark green, salmon, purple, salmon terra-cotta, and black paint
- Protective clear coat (water-based)
- 31–6" x 6" unglazed tiles
- ¼" toothed mastic spreader
- Mastic (tile glue)
- Grout
- Sponge
- Rags for grout cleanup
- Silicon spray to seal grout
- Plywood, at least ¾" thick, to mount tiles. This project used a sheet 28" x 40".
- Tack cloth
- 1½" molding
- Finishing nails

Leslie and I were scheduled to give a stenciling seminar in San Diego, and as usual, we were running behind and frantically finishing projects so we could photograph them for our slide show. The tiled table pictured here was one of the projects under construction. The slide of the table turned out very well. To our audience, sitting in a hot, crowded conference room in mid-July, Leslie's table, shown in a lush garden setting and offering white wine, looked very inviting. The truth is, the table was balanced precariously on makeshift legs, and the beverage was fishpond water. Since then, the tabletop has acquired proper legs and found a home in Leslie's backyard under her grape arbor.

METHOD

1. Using a trowel or spreader, scoop out the mastic (or "tile glue") onto your plywood surface. Spread it over the surface in an even coat using a ¼" toothed mastic spreader.
2. Seven of the tiles were cut into 2" x 6" strips and two were cut into 2" x 2" squares to fill gaps in the border. There will be one 2" x 4" piece left over.
3. Lay out the tiles according to the diagram provided.
4. Place tiles together in your pattern, leaving ¹⁄₁₆" to ⅛" of an inch between tiles. You can purchase spacers to help you get even spaces between the tiles. The glue will take time to set which will allow you

See page 40 for details on
STANDARD TOOLS & MATERIALS

time to adjust the spacing and arrangement of your tiles.

5. Allow the glue to dry and harden at least for 24 hours before beginning to paint.

6. Using painter's tape, mask the border of tiles going around the outside. These border tiles will be left natural except for the clear coat applied in Step 15. The tape acts as a mask to ensure the border tiles aren't painted.

7. Lightly roughen your 6" x 6" tiles by sanding them with 120 grit sandpaper. Clean off any dust with a tack cloth and then basecoat these tiles with a primer applied using a brush or roller. Allow to dry according to manufacturer's directions.

8. Paint the background colors with two standard 2" paintbrushes. Using horizontal brush strokes, start at the top with a very light sky blue. Halfway down change brushes and paint, switching to a very light green applied with horizontal strokes. The colors are so pale they are easily blended. You may wish to add glaze to facilitate blending. Let dry overnight.

9. Draw a 24" x 36" rectangle with a permanent felt marker on your freezer paper. Then spray repositionable spray adhesive on the matte side of the freezer paper and place the paper on the wall.

10. Project the flower and pot design to fit the rectangle on the paper and trace the image.

11. Place the pattern on your tabletop. Following the color key provided, begin to cut out the shapes and

stencil your tiles.

12. *Note*: Unglazed tiles are very tough on blades, so be prepared to go through four or five while cutting out the image. Start by cutting out all the medium green leaves. Use a stencil roller and let the paint dry. When the paint is dry, add purple highlights at the tips of the leaves using a ⅝" stencil brush. Make sure to use a dry brush technique so your paint doesn't bleed. Cut out dark green stems using ⅝" stencil brush. Stencil these cutouts dark green.

13. Next, cut out the flowers. Stencil them blue at the tips, and fade into salmon at their bases. See Chapter 1 for more information on shading and blending and using extenders.

14. Cut out the pot, and with a roller stencil it terra-cotta. Let the paint dry and then, using a ⅝" stencil brush, shade with black around the outside of the pot to give the illusion of roundness. Remove all the freezer paper and the painter's tape.

15. Leslie added the dragonfly from Buckingham Stencils last. You can use any other commercial or handmade stencil you like.

16. If the table is to be used outside, it is important to protect it with an exterior clear coat. The exterior coating should be applied several times.

17. Let the final coat dry for 24 hours and then fill between the tiles with grout, according to the manufacturer's directions.

18. To complete the table, finish the rough ¾" plywood edges by gluing, then nailing, 1½" strips of molding to the sides of your table. These four pieces should be stained or painted and cut to fit mitered corners.

19. Serve drinks on the terrace and have everyone over to admire your handiwork!

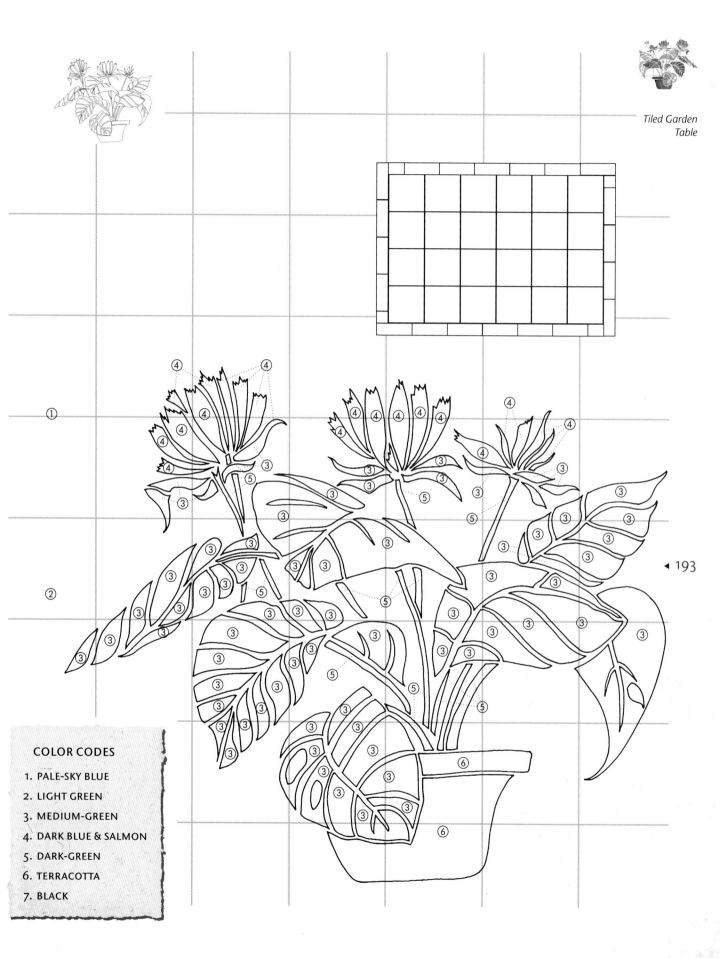

Tiled Garden
Table

◄ 193

COLOR CODES

1. PALE-SKY BLUE

2. LIGHT GREEN

3. MEDIUM-GREEN

4. DARK BLUE & SALMON

5. DARK-GREEN

6. TERRACOTTA

7. BLACK

Glass "Etched" Fish & Kelp

Stenciling on Glass

Last summer we sold our family home and moved aboard a 46-foot motor cruiser. Our new home, *Inside Passage*, is a replica of a 1920s rum-runner. She is a finely fitted yacht with a splendid mahogany interior, but when I looked around for walls to stencil, there weren't any! To me, a home isn't a home without stenciling. So, lacking walls to stencil, I turned to windows, mirrors, and cabinet glass. Now etched glass abounds in our vintage vessel. But our boat isn't really vintage, it's a reproduction, and the windows, mirrors, and cabinet doors aren't really etched, they are (you guessed it) stenciled!

I "etched" our glass using Delta's PermEnamel Glass Etching Paint Kit, and the result is indistinguishable from the real thing.

METHOD

The following method for stenciling the seascape mirror, the washday window, the cabinet doors, and the herons is one and the same.

1. Clean the glass with glass cleaner, rinse, and dry thoroughly.
2. Once you have traced your design onto freezer paper and sprayed the back of the paper with spray glue, position the paper on the glass.
3. With your X-acto® or utility knife, cut out the design, and remove all

SPECIAL TOOLS & MATERIALS

- Delta's PermEnamel Glass Etching Paint Kit
- One stencil roller

See page 40 for details on
STANDARD TOOLS & MATERIALS

paper pieces in the design where you wish the etching to appear.

4. Using the small sponge from the Etching Paint Kit, apply a coat of the PermEnamel Surface Conditioner through the openings in the designs. Dry the conditioner with a hairdryer.

5. Use a stencil roller and roller stenciling technique to roll on a coat of PermEnamel White Frost. Dry this with a hairdryer and then apply a second coat.

6. Let the paint dry for ten days before washing. Do not clean with harsh abrasives.

Note: "Etching" can be removed with a razor blade should you decide to update your décor.

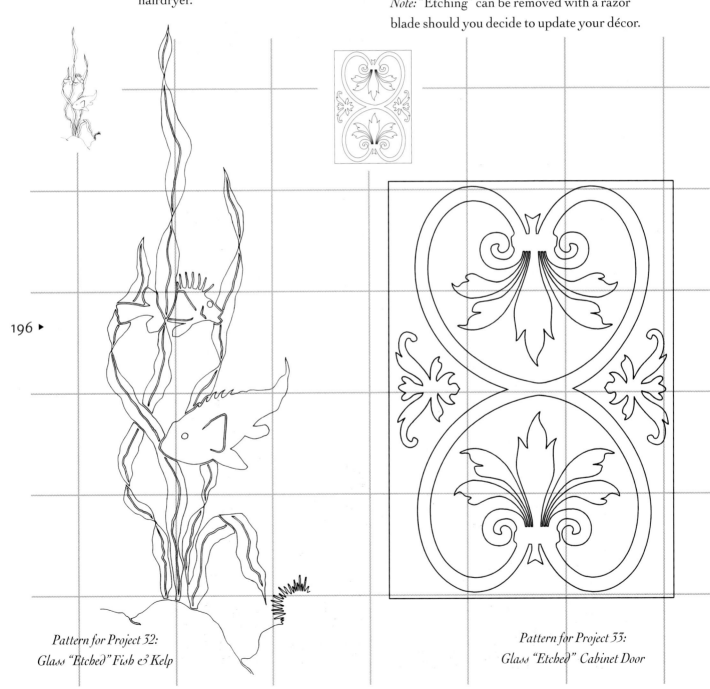

Pattern for Project 32:
Glass "Etched" Fish & Kelp

Pattern for Project 33:
Glass "Etched" Cabinet Door

Glass "Etched" Cabinet Door

See *Project 32:*
Glass "Etched"
Fish & Kelp for
details on
TOOLS & MATERIALS
AND METHOD

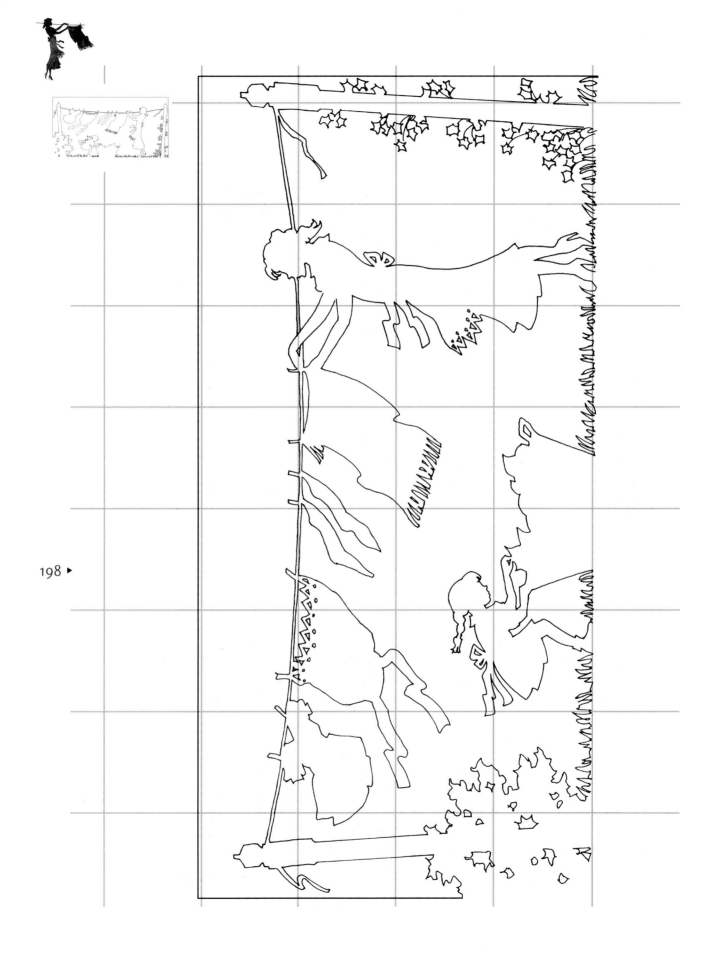

PROJECT 34

Glass "Etched" Window

◀ 199

See *Project 32: Glass "Etched" Fish & Kelp* for details on **TOOLS & MATERIALS AND METHOD**

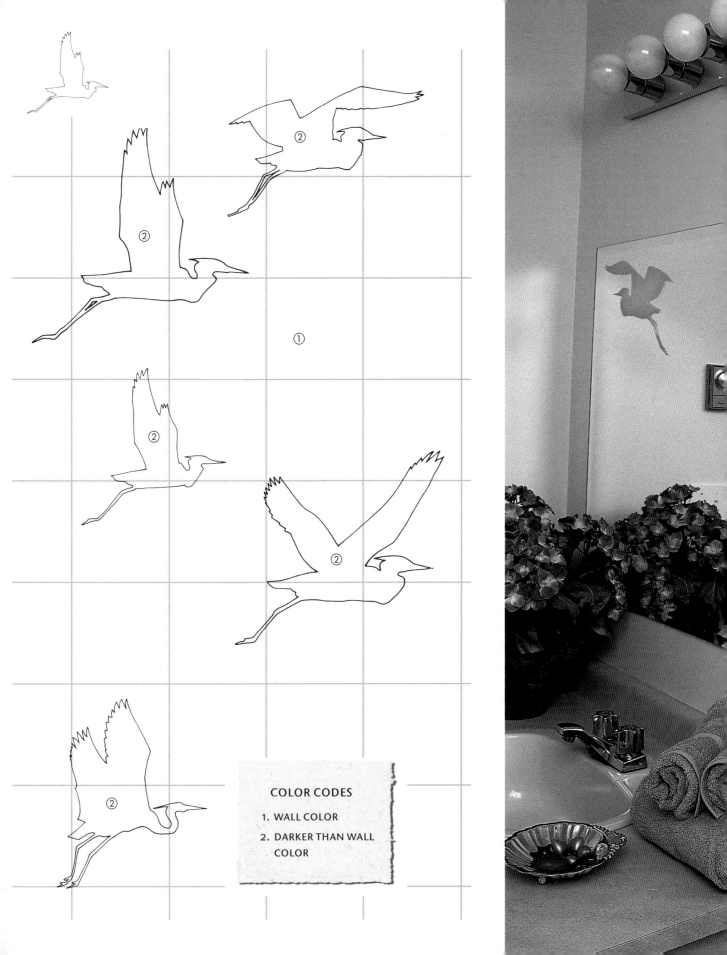

COLOR CODES

1. WALL COLOR
2. DARKER THAN WALL COLOR

Glass "Etched" Herons

See *Project 32:*
Glass "Etched"
Fish & Kelp for details on
TOOLS & MATERIALS AND METHOD

PROJECT 36

Christmas Clip Art

It was June when we painted the Santa pictured here on Leslie's front door as a project for this book. To get us in the mood for the project we played Christmas carols and sang along off key. It is a good thing Leslie lives on secluded acreage with no neighbors in sight or hearing distance, because they would be sure to wonder if we had gotten into the Christmas grog much, much too early.

Clip art is a great source for projection stenciling ideas, and because the designs are often quite simple, they are perfect for holiday murals. Your holiday mural will only be around a brief time (unless you are one of those people who still has Christmas lights up in July), so you don't want to make painting it a life's work.

We used Jo Sonja's acrylic paints for our window painting because they gave even opaque coverage and adhered well to the glass.

METHOD

1. Cut out the horn and the star and roller stencil them golden yellow. It will take a couple of coats of paint to get good coverage. You may speed up the drying time by using a hairdryer. Once the paint has dried, replace the horn and star cutouts.
2. Cut out the two parts of the Christmas tree and roller them green. Replace these cutouts once the paint has dried.

◄ 203

SPECIAL TOOLS & MATERIALS

- One stencil roller and five refills
- Two ½" stencil brushes
- Jo Sonja's acrylic paint in red, white, black, primary green, yellow oxide, and golden yellow

See page 40 for details on
STANDARD TOOLS & MATERIALS

3. Cut out the red sections of Santa's suit and roller stencil them red. Replace these cutouts once the paint has dried.

4. Cut out the mouths and eyes of the Santa and horse and save these cutouts. Use a stencil brush to stencil these openings black, and replace their cutouts to act as a mask once the black paint dries.

5. Cut out all the white sections of the design and roller stencil them white. Make sure not to wipe the smile off Santa's face, by leaving its mask in place.

6. Cut out the hobby horse and remove this cutout, being careful to leave the eye and mouth mask in place. Roller stencil the hobby horse terra-cotta.

7. Cut out Santa's face (which includes Santa's nose), once again being careful not to disturb the eye masks, and roller stencil the face light pink.

Once this paint dries, replace the face cutout and cut out Santa's nose. Using a stencil brush, shade around the outside of his nose with red and rub a little color into his cheeks.

8. Remove all the freezer paper and bring in the grog to add a little color to your cheeks.

204 ▶

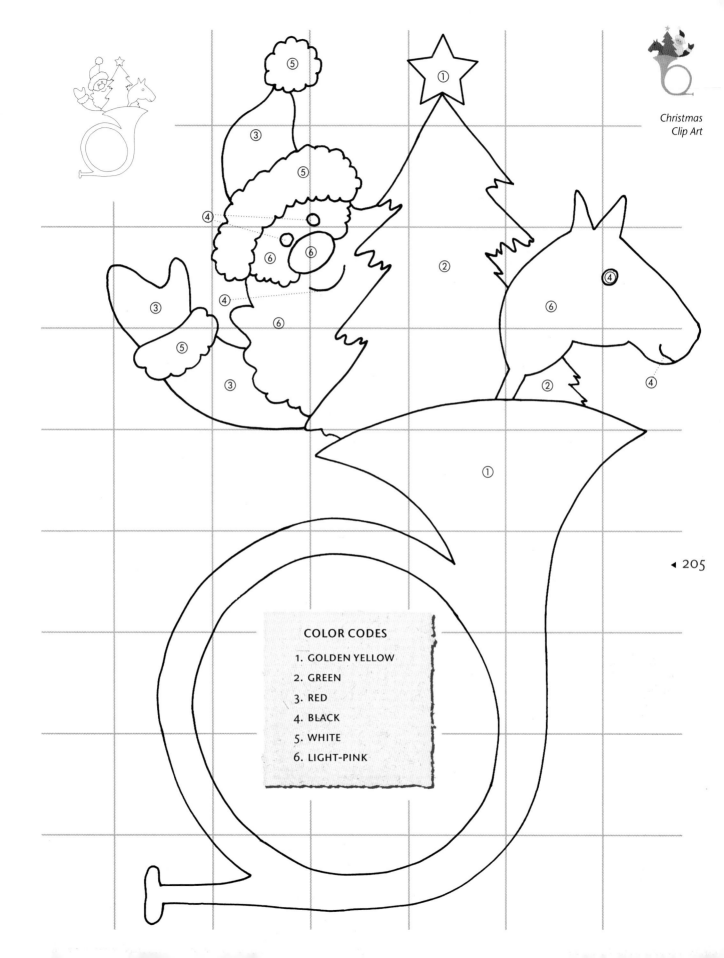

⑤
③
⑤
④
⑤
⑥
⑥
①
②
④
⑥
④
④
③
④
⑥
⑥
②
①
③
⑤
②
④
①

◄ 205

COLOR CODES

1. GOLDEN YELLOW
2. GREEN
3. RED
4. BLACK
5. WHITE
6. LIGHT-PINK

The Unstenciled Stencil

We call this stencil the "unstenciled stencil" because that is what it is. The stencil is cut out of MacTac, or its more durable cousin, sign vinyl. No paint is applied. You are done. The openings in the stencil make up the design.

We used the unstenciled stencil on a porthole in our head aboard *Inside Passage*. The frosted nature of the vinyl afforded us needed privacy and the sailboats cut into the vinyl gave our porthole a custom etched look. Down the road, or down the channel as the case may be, if we want to change the design, or wish to have no design at all, we can simply peel the vinyl away.

The downside of the unstenciled stencil is that Leslie and I have developed a nasty habit. Whenever we see what appears to be etched glass, be it an elegant design in a restaurant window, or lettering and a logo at a legal office, we have to submit it to a little thumbnail test. We have discovered that there is a whole subculture of unstenciled stencils out there!

METHOD

1. The first step is to apply frosted MacTac or sign vinyl to your clean, dry window surface.
2. Cut your MacTac generously, and trim in place with your utility knife.

SPECIAL TOOLS & MATERIALS

- Frosted MacTac or frosted sign vinyl (available at hardware stores, art supply stores, sign shops, and some drugstores)
- Buckingham Sailpast border
- Glass window or panel
- Stencil brush or roller
- Paint in any color

See page 40 for details on
STANDARD TOOLS & MATERIALS

LIGHT HOUSEKEEPING

3. Photocopy your design, apply repositionable spray adhesive to the back of this photocopy and affix it to the vinyl on your window.

4. Using your X-acto® or utility knife, cut out the sailboats, cutting through the photocopy and through the vinyl, and remove these cutouts.

6. Once all the boats are cut out, remove only the freezer paper to reveal your "etched" window.

Note: We used the sailboat motifs taken from Buckingham Stencils' Sailpast border (on the previous page) and the lighthouse pattern opposite for the light housekeeping sign (on this page).

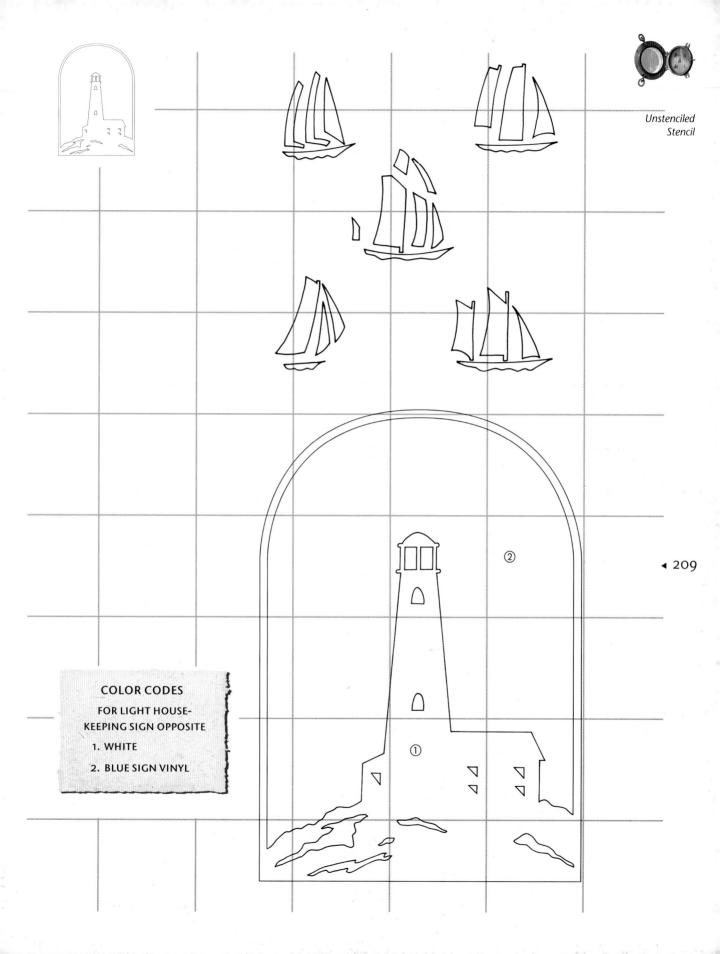

COLOR CODES
FOR LIGHT HOUSE-
KEEPING SIGN OPPOSITE
1. WHITE
2. BLUE SIGN VINYL

Art Nouveau Floor Arts
Fabulous Floors

SPECIAL TOOLS & MATERIALS

- 220 grit sandpaper
- A piece of linoleum, at least 4' x 6'
- Natural sea sponge
- Latex glaze
- Painter's tape
- Five stencil rollers (or one roller and four foam re-fills)
- One or two ½" stencil brushes
- Two low-pile nap rollers for primer and base coat
- 100% acrylic white primer
- Water-based or oil-based protective clearcoat acrylic
- Water-based glaze
- Golden yellow latex in a semigloss for base coat
- light blue, dark blue, golden yellow, orange-red, blue, white, and blue-green paint

*T*he Art Nouveau period extended from about 1880 to 1910. The style lends itself to projection stenciling due to the stylized, graphic, three-dimensional images it is famous for. Art Nouveau is very versatile. The colors can be muted or vibrant and the designs can be painted almost anywhere, including stairways, walls, lampshades, furniture, and even dinnerware.

Leslie used the reverse side of a piece of linoleum with a cardboard-type backing for this design to create a quick, easy, non-traditional floorcloth. The reverse side gives you an open canvas to paint on. Linoleum can easily be cut into any shape or trimmed to fit around furniture or fixtures. Linoleum lies flat and will not turn up at the sides or corners. It can be held in place with two-sided carpet tape, it doesn't need to be hemmed, and it resists cracking and fold lines.

Pieces of linoleum can be found inexpensively as remnants. Leslie found a 9' x 6' piece in a secondhand shop for only three dollars. Look for a fairly thick piece as it will wear longer.

METHOD

1. Cut your linoleum to the desired size. Lightly sand the cut edges to smooth out any rough areas. Paint the underside of your linoleum

See page 40 for details on
STANDARD TOOLS & MATERIALS

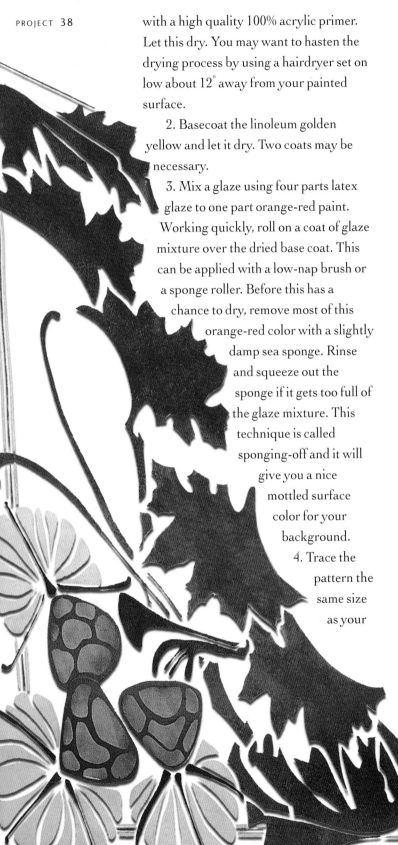

with a high quality 100% acrylic primer. Let this dry. You may want to hasten the drying process by using a hairdryer set on low about 12" away from your painted surface.

2. Basecoat the linoleum golden yellow and let it dry. Two coats may be necessary.

3. Mix a glaze using four parts latex glaze to one part orange-red paint. Working quickly, roll on a coat of glaze mixture over the dried base coat. This can be applied with a low-nap brush or a sponge roller. Before this has a chance to dry, remove most of this orange-red color with a slightly damp sea sponge. Rinse and squeeze out the sponge if it gets too full of the glaze mixture. This technique is called sponging-off and it will give you a nice mottled surface color for your background.

4. Trace the pattern the same size as your

"carpet" onto freezer paper and then place the freezer paper on top of your linoleum once the topcoat has dried.

5. Using a sharp utility knife cut out all the orange-red leaves from the freezer paper pattern. Remove these pieces and discard. Roller stencil these areas orange-red. Let the paint dry.

6. Next cut out all the white sections of the flowers. You will need several coats of white for good coverage. Remove and discard the cutouts. Using a roller stencil, paint these areas white. Let the paint dry.

7. Next cut out all the dark blue branches. Remove the cutouts and discard. Using a stencil brush and dry brush technique, paint these areas dark blue.

8. Cut out and remove the triangular mushroom shapes under the white flowers. Save the cutouts. Using a stencil roller or brush, paint these areas blue-green. Let the paint dry and replace these cutouts.

9. Cut out the blue shapes inside the mushroom shape. Discard the cutouts and stencil these areas light blue using a stencil brush. Remove all the freezer paper. Using painters' tape to define the areas, paint in the orange-red borders, then the white border. Let them dry overnight before proceeding to the next step.

10. For the final step, apply an acrylic clearcoat spray to the entire surface. I recommend four to five coats with the requisite drying time between them.

COLOR CODES

1. ORANGE-RED
2. WHITE
3. DARK-BLUE
4. BLUE-GREEN
5. LIGHT-BLUE

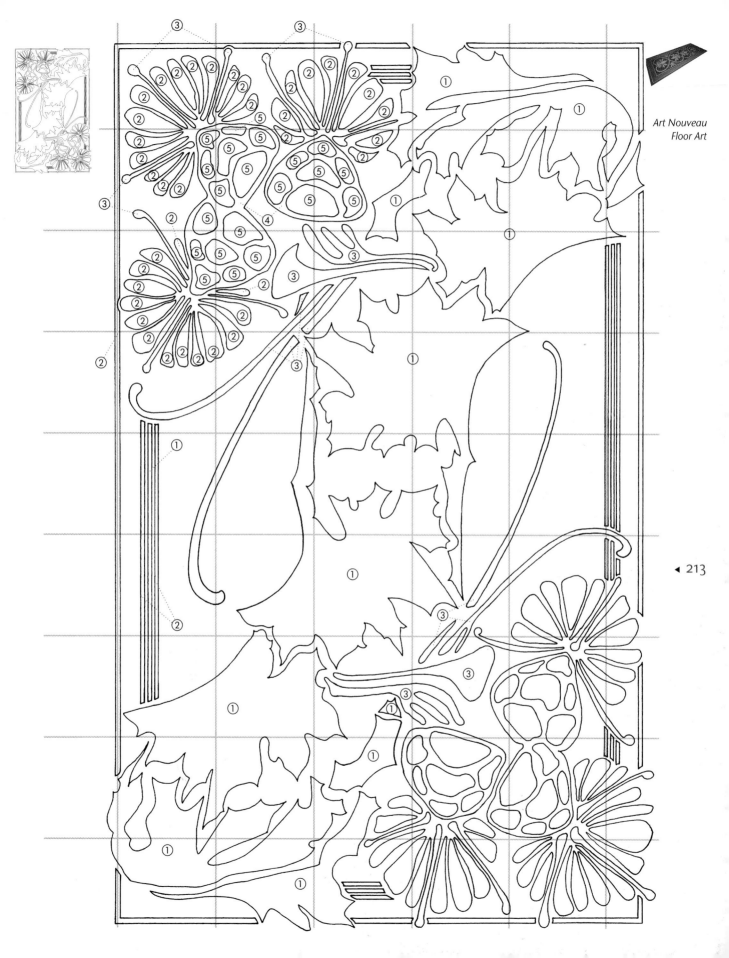

◄ 213

Don't Take it for Granite!

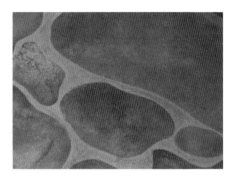

SPECIAL TOOLS & MATERIALS

- Three or four stencil rollers (or one roller and four refills)
- Three or four ½," ⅝ " and 1" stencil brushes
- Feather or sword liner or artist's liner brush
- Soft bristled paint brush
- Water-based glaze
- Stir sticks
- Small plastic containers for several paint/glaze mixtures
- Cheese cloth
- Sea sponge
- Cardboard
- Plastic wrap
- Newspaper
- Hard-wearing paint such as a porch and floor paint for base coat
- Gray, light gray, dark gray, rust, terra-cotta, black, white, light tan, dark tan, taupe, yellow-ochre, and light mauve paint
- Clearcoat (water-based)

Leslie painted a faux river rock floor at a fish hatchery. She enjoyed watching the reactions of visitors to the hatchery who were amazed that rock could be sliced so thin and flat.

Great areas for faux stone work include entrance halls, sunrooms, patios, fireplace walls, hot tub or bathtub surrounds, or staircase landings, as Leslie did here. You can also stencil faux brickwork, paving stones, and flagstones. Stencil them in colors that will complement your décor.

There are more freehand techniques involved with this project than most of the others. Think of it as a mini course in using different tools to create a variety of finishes.

As with any flooring project, don't paint yourself into a corner. There is nothing more boring than being trapped in a corner of a room and watching paint dry.

METHOD

1. Paint the floor gray (or any color you want to show through as your grout). Let the paint dry. Follow your paint dealer's advice when it comes to repairing, stripping, sanding, and priming your floor.
2. Randomly sponge on light gray using a large damp sea sponge. This will give your background an interesting texture. If your floor is in

See page 40 for details on
STANDARD TOOLS & MATERIALS

poor condition, this paint treatment is an ideal way to hide flaws. Let it dry 24 hours before proceeding

3. Measure the floor area to be stenciled. Place the freezer paper on a wall, using repositionable spray adhesive. Project and trace the pattern onto the paper so it covers the desired measured area. If you have an area too large to cover with the projected image, the pattern has been designed so that you can flip it over and continue it in any direction on the floor. This will give the pattern variety and interest.

4. Place the rock pattern on the floor to be stenciled. Use the painter's tape around the outside of the freezer paper pattern to hold it in place. Cut out and paint the rocks one at a time, painting them with one or a combination of stone finishes listed below. Let each "rock" dry and replace its cutout before beginning the rock next to it.

5. When all the rocks are done, remove the freezer paper.

6. Allow the painted rocks to dry overnight, then roll or brush on a protective clearcoat. Let this coat dry thoroughly, then repeat. Apply three to four layers of clearcoat (we used Varathane Diamond-coat water-based semigloss) and sand between final coats.

ROCK FINISHES

Note: All the paint/glaze mixtures are made by adding one part paint to one part glaze.

Granite

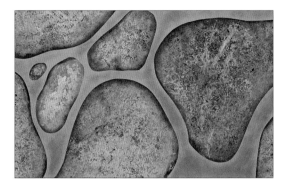

To create faux granite, stencil the rock shape light gray. Let the paint dry. Pour four pools of paint/glaze mixture in black, white, medium gray (a combination of black and white), and terra-cotta onto a single paint palette. Take a large damp sea sponge and press it lightly into the paint mixtures at random. Dab sponge on a paper towel to test imprint. Generally, you should see different amounts of all four colors on your sponge at once with some overlapping of color. Once you are satisfied with the imprint on the paper towel, press the sea sponge onto the light gray base through the cutout. Don't let too much paint/glaze mixture accumulate on your sponge. This will help prevent paint from bleeding under your stencil. If you wish to blend your colors, take a dry stencil roller and run it gently over the surface of the rock. Shade dark gray around the edges of the rock. Change color balances by varying how much of each color you pick up on your sponge.

Sedimentary Rock

To create faux sedimentary rock, stencil the rock shape a light color, using a stencil roller. With a ¼" bristle brush and wavy strokes, pull a mixture of paint and glaze across the rock pattern. Immediately, while the first streak is still wet, pull another color across. Repeat this until you have four or five different paint/glaze mixtures crossing the rock in irregular bands of color. Using a piece of non-corrugated cardboard that has been torn straight across to give a somewhat straight edge, drag across the still-wet bands of color in a soft wavy line.

Repeat these bands (varying the color combinations) until the rock is complete. With a ⅝" stencil brush and dark gray paint, shade around the outside of the rock.

Unpolished Stone

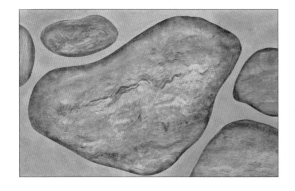

To create unpolished stone, use a stencil roller to stencil the rock a light color. To create the texture of the stone finish, apply with a stencil roller a darker paint/glaze mixture over the entire surface. Take a piece of newspaper that has been crumpled up and then spread open and place it over the wet paint/glaze mixture. "Smoosh" or press the newspaper onto the surface using the palms of your hands to vary the pressure. Most newspapers will leave black smudges which will enhance the "texture" of the rock. When dry shade dark gray around the outside of the rock using a ⅝" stencil brush. You can use other tools to "smoosh" as well, including plastic bags, brown paper bags, and plastic wrap, to name just a few. Have fun and experiment!

Veining

To create veins in your rocks, use a feather or a swordliner brush to drag a one part paint/one part glaze/two parts water mixture across your rock as a final touch. Make your lines diagonal but be careful not to end your veins in "V"s. Twist, turn, pull and push the feather to create a variety of veins. Use a cheesecloth to lightly blot the veins. Hold a paint brush (any old soft bristle or synthetic brush will do) perpendicular to the surface and drag it lightly across the wet veins at right angles to the veins in one direction and occasionally in the opposite direction or in the same direction as the veins. This softens and diffuses the veins as well as "pushes" them into the surface.

The Lizard

A great addition to any room is the lizard. Place him in an inconspicuous spot so that he can surprise people. Leslie recalls stenciling an elaborate garden room mural in a showroom bathroom. The lush scene took days of hard work. Just for fun, she decided to hide a tiny frog behind some foliage in a corner. When the developer came in to view the completed work her first remark had absolutely nothing to do with the garden scene. She exclaimed, "Oh, what a cute little frog!"

The lizard also looks appealing above a sill of a doorway, outside on entrance steps, or grouped around a child's room in many different colors.

METHOD

1. Cut around the outside of the lizard's body. Remove this cutout and set it aside. Basecoat the lizard's body yellow-green. Let the paint dry.

2. To give the lizard a mottled, multi-colored appearance, use stencil brushes to pounce or blend rust and dark green paint onto him. Round out his body by shading around it using dark green. Let the paint dry.

3. Reposition the body and cut out the eye. Remove this cutout and paint the exposed area bright yellow. Alternatively, you can use the "wrong" end of a small artist's brush or stencil brush to dab on a spot of yellow for the eye. Remove the freezer papel the lizard and stand back to wait for - reactions.

218

SPECIAL TOOLS & MATERIALS

- Yellow-green, rust, yellow, and dark green paint
- Three or four stencil brushes in ⅝" and ½" sizes

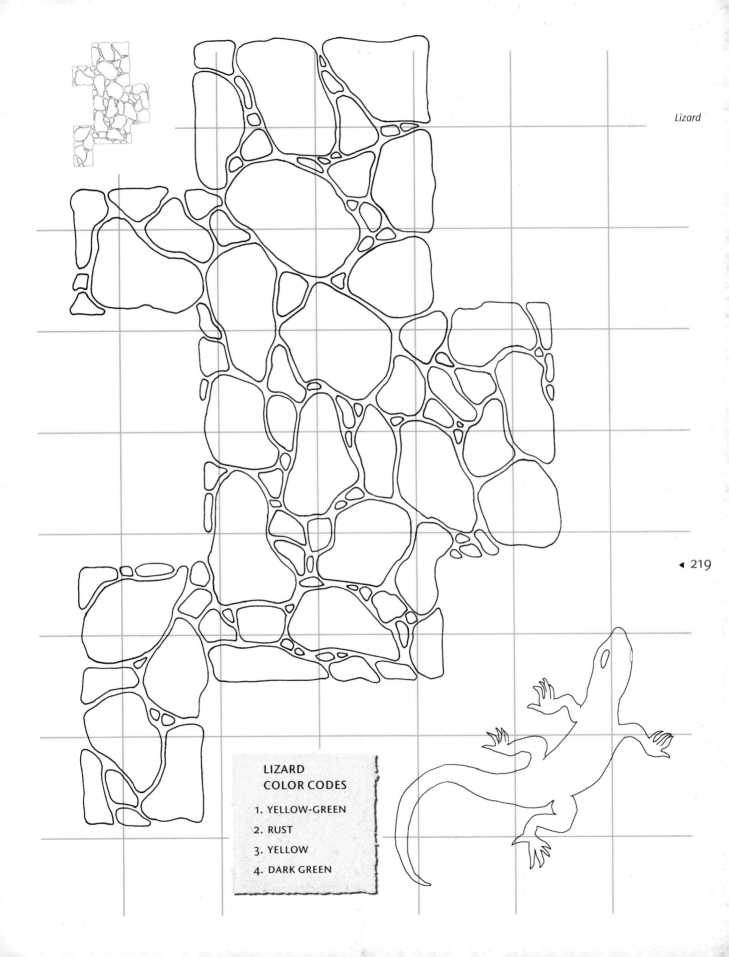

◄ 219

**LIZARD
COLOR CODES**

1. YELLOW-GREEN

2. RUST

3. YELLOW

4. DARK GREEN

Victorian Floorcloth

*F*loorcloths are painted canvas floor coverings. They were - popular in 18th-century Europe where they were used as decora tive alternatives to rugs. Often these floor coverings were stenciled. For early settlers in North America, floorcloths were often the only covering over the clay or dirt floors in their homes. Today the main appeal of a floorcloth is aesthetic. Its hand-made charm makes it an attractive alternative to vinyl floor covering and because it is hand-crafted, it can be fashioned into any size, shape, design, or color.

Aboard our boat, *Inside Passage*, the appeal of the floorcloth is more than just aesthetic. In a marine environment, once something gets damp, it often wants to stay that way. For that reason I was very happy to replace the carpet runner in my galley with a floorcloth. Floorcloths are perfect for boats. They are durable, waterproof, and easy to clean, and because they are made of canvas they are just right for nautical décor.

METHOD

1. Before you begin to paint your floorcloth, cut off the selvages to prevent wrinkling or shrinking of the canvas as it dries. Allow a 1" margin around the outside of your floorcloth. This margin will later be folded under to create a hem.

SPECIAL TOOLS & MATERIALS

- #10 weight canvas
- White primer or gesso (if canvas is not primed)
- Painter's tape
- Measuring tape
- White all-purpose glue
- Stencil rollers
- Stencil brushes
- Green, burgundy, and metallic gold paint
- Urethane or varnish
- Very fine sandpaper

See page 40 for details on
STANDARD TOOLS & MATERIALS

2. Stretch the canvas taut and secure it in place by stapling, tacking, or duct-taping it to a floor, tabletop, piece of plywood or drywall, or whatever convenient place you can find to stencil it.

3. Our floorcloth was #10 weight primed canvas but if your canvas is not primed, this is the time to do it. For priming use a good quality primer or gesso. Let the primer dry overnight.

4. Apply the base coat. Basecoat the entire floorcloth using burgundy paint. Once the base coat has dried, stencil the green and gold borders using painter's tape to define the areas to be stenciled. It will take several coats of paint to build up the desired color intensity.

5. Measure the interior burgundy rectangle, and draw an identical rectangle on freezer paper. Using repositionable spray adhesive, fix the freezer paper to your wall so you can project the Victorian design onto it for tracing. Once traced, take the freezer paper off the wall and carefully position it on the floorcloth for cutting. Cut out the pattern and, using a roller, stencil the exposed areas with gold paint. Again, it will take several coats of paint to get the richness of color you are after.

6. After the stenciling has dried, crease along your one-inch margin, fold the margin under, and miter the corners (fold them and cut them diagonally to eliminate bulk). Glue the hem down with white all-purpose glue, then press it firmly with a rolling pin or heavy bottle (we keep bottles of wine in the studio just for this purpose!) to flatten the hem and to distribute the glue evenly.

Allow the hemmed edges to dry overnight before applying finish coats.

7. Cover the canvas with at least three coats of varnish or urethane (check manufacturer's instructions for paint compatibility), allowing adequate drying time between coats.

8. To minimize the possibility of the finished floorcloth sliding on the floor, spray a little repositionable stencil adhesive on the back of it. Allow the spray glue to dry well before placing the floorcloth on the floor for use.

9. After it is finished and the paint and varnish have cured, the floorcloth can be wiped clean with warm, soapy water. Never fold a floorcloth since this encourages cracking. If you need to move it or store it, roll it around a cylinder to prevent its surface from cracking. Treat it like the work of art it is! Floorcloths are very durable and perfect for hardwood floors.

• For the pattern please see *Project 35: Glass "Etched" Cabinet Door* on page 196.

COLOR CODES

BERGUNDY, GREEN AND METALLIC GOLD

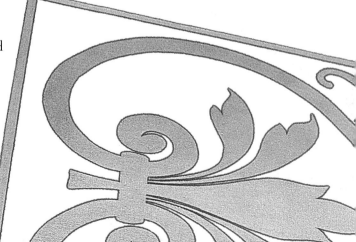

Sources

Where to find supplies

The following is a list of tools and materials we used in the production of the projects in this book. Most of these items are available from art supply stores, home décor stores, specialty paint stores, hardware stores, and office supply stores. Check out the telephone directory under paint, craft supplies, or art supplies to find a local source. You could also visit our Internet site: www.projections-tenciling.com

Stencil supplies

Stencil supplies, including craft acrylic paints, glazes, repositionable stencil spray adhesive, stenciling rollers, stencil brushes, and paint palettes are widely available at craft and hobby stores, paint outlets, and home decorating centers. *Note:* Stencils and stencil supplies were almost exclusively done using Buckingham Stencil Products. These included stencils brushes, positionable spray adhesive, stencil rollers and refills, Buckingham roller stencil paint, paint palettes and Blending Glaze. A variety of Buckingham commercial precut laser stencils were used to complement a few of the projects. These include:

Dragonfly on the Tile Table Page 191

Blossom stencil, flower pots, in the Cottage Window Page 153

European Cave Art as described on page 39

Terracotta clay pot, Leafy Branch, Ivy, Morning Glory, Iris, Fern, Blossom, and Clematis used with the Arbor on page 137.

Buckingham products

CANADA

Retail Stores

Paint stores and selected art, craft and decorative painting shops.

Mail Order

Projection Stenciling 1-877-301-8181

Mary Maxim 1-888-442-2266

Cheshire Cat 1-888-678-3233

UNITED STATES

Retail Stores

Selected Michael's store and selected arts, craft, and decorative painting shops

Mail Order

Stenciler's Emporium 1-800-229-1760

The Bernardo-Leal Stencil Co.
    1-508-823-0851

Secure On-Line Ordering

Projection Stenciling
    www.projectionstenciling.com

Paints

Latex and craft acrylic paints are available from hobby shops, paint stores and art supply stores.

Projectors

Available for rent at low cost from office supply shops, photography shops, community centers. Check also with friends.

Tracer and Jr. Tracers

Artograph
    2838 Vicksburg Lane
    North Plymouth, MN 55447
    Tel: 612-553-1112
    www.rexart.com/artograph

Glass Etching Kit

Delta Technical Coatings
    2550 Pellisier Place
    Whittier, CA 90501
    Tel: 1-800-423-4135
    www.deltacrafts.com

◄ 223

Freezer Paper

Local supermarkets or meat packing companies.
Patina Paints: Moderns Options
    2325 3rd St.
    San Francisco, CA 94107
    Tel: 415-252-5580
    www.ModernOptions.com

Painters' Tape

Available from paint and hardware stores.
Brands:
Painter's Mate Delicate®
Kleen Edge®

Sign Vinyl

Art supply stores, sign printers.

Chalkboard Paint

Paint stores and selected craft shops.
Chromacryl Student Acrylics for Xmas window mural:
    Chroma 205 Bucky Drive
    Lititz, PA 17543
    Tel: 1-800-257-8278
    www.chroma-inc.com

Permanent Felt Markers

Stationery stores, art supply stores.

Utility knives and X-acto® knives

Art supply stores, hardware stores.

Resources

Projection Stenciling Video with Linda Buckingham and Leslie Bird, call Projection Stenciling 1-877-301-8181 or for on-line ordering www.projectionstenciling.com

    The Art of Stencilling Video with Sandra and Linda Buckingham, Buckingham Stencils Inc.

    Stencilling — A Harrowsmith Guide, by Sandra Buckingham, Firefly Books.

    Stencilling on a Grand Scale, by Sandra Buckingham, Firefly Books.

    The Stencil Artisans League, Inc. 1900 Arch Street. Philadelphia, PA 19103-1498, tel (215) 564-3484 or Web www.sali.org SALI is a non-profit international organization dedicated to the promotion of stenciling and decorative painting. If you would like additional information on stenciling products, instruction, seminars, and local stenciling groups contact SALI to become a member and receive their quarterly magazine.